Never Let The Facts Interfere With A Good Story

by
JUDY D.V. HARLES

Published in the United States by
The Vega Group.
Tinley Park, IL 60477
vegaunleashed.com

ePub ISBN: 979-8-9886660-2-8
Paperback ISBN: 979-8-9886660-1-1

ᗞEDICATION

Gerry is dead, because of Parkinson's, and Lewy Body Dementia (LBD). His life ended as he lived, doing it his way. He had a big life, too big to be contained in just one book, even though I promised our children I would write one as a celebration of his life. So, this book is about the first ten years of our life together. But in recounting his life, I found I must include my experiences as well.

"When you meet the one who changes the way your heart beats, dance with them to that rhythm for as long as the song lasts" (Kirk Diedrich). For "once in a while, right in the middle of an ordinary life-love gives us a fairy tale." (Langford Beard). Our dance, our fairy tale, lasted for 52 years!

Death changes everything! Time changes nothing! I still miss the sound of his voice, the wisdom of his advice, the stories of our life, just being in his presence. So, no, time changes nothing. I miss him as much as I did the day he died.

This book is for you, Gerry.

TABLE OF CONTENTS

"Meet Cute"

I guess since I am going to recount the story of how I met Gerry that spring of 1967, I should really begin by telling you how I ended up on a boat in the middle of the Mediterranean Sea headed for India by way of Turkey with less than $100 in my purse. I was 20 years old and had left Florence and the *Università per stranieri* with my parents' permission, with the intention of seeing as much of Asia as my wits, my funds, and my thumb could take me.

So, where do I begin? Well, I was born in Lake Forest, Illinois. No. I'm not going to recount all 20 years, just highlights that perhaps destined me for that boat in 1967. Anyway, I was born on my mother's 27th birthday. The hospital made a big deal about this fact. Not only was this special, but back in the day, 27-year-old women were considered 'old' to be having a first child.

After the celebrations were over and the cake was cleared away, one catty nurse commented, "Well, Mrs. Vignocchi, you certainly waited a long time to have your first child."

My mother guilelessly replied, "Not really. I won't be married nine months until tomorrow."

My father always pointed out that I was premature, but that part of the story was always buried in the laughs over my mother's clever retort.

The first real memory I have was when we were living in Highland Park, Illinois. I was five years old, and our family was expecting another baby. I really wanted a sister. I already had two brothers and felt outnumbered, even though I was the eldest. My school was above the church, and every afternoon after school, I would stop at the church and say a prayer, asking for a sister.

That summer, my prayers were answered. Soon, I realized the consequence to the prayers was that I was no longer the treasured little girl! Now, this I do not remember, but my mother tells the story that in the fall after first grade, I continued to pray at the church every day. When the nuns asked my mother if she was again expecting and she replied that she was not, they asked me what I was praying for. Having had success with my first round of prayers, I decided to try again. I blithely told them that I was asking God to take back my sister and exchange her for another brother!

Of course, it didn't work; the eldest remained my only designation. In addition to the sister that I couldn't return, my parents had two more boys and another sister for a total of seven children.

My father was 100% Italian, and my mother was Welch, Scottish, English, Cherokee Indian, and as a joke, a little bit alligator. Growing up, we just simplified the matter by telling everyone we were half Italian.

I was quite close to my Nono (grandpa in Italian). He lived with us until he passed away. When I was seven years old, my parents bought a house in Lake Forest and made the decision to start me in the new school for second grade. My father drove me to school every day, and after school, one of the nuns would walk me to the train station, where I would catch the train home. Halfway home, the train stopped in Highwood, where my Nono would go to visit with his friends daily as this is the town that he and all his friends immigrated to after being processed through Ellis Island. We were known on that train as the

"Old Man and the Little Girl" and always got a seat. In our talks on that train, I always told Nono that one day I would go to Italy.

When I was in college, I studied Italian, and was shocked at how easy it was that first semester.

When I came home for Thanksgiving holiday, I told my father and he laughed and said, "Wait till you get to words you did not learn from Nono." Darn it, he was right!

At the beginning of my sophomore year at the University of Illinois where I majored in political science, I found a college in Florence, Italy, that was reasonably priced, and asked my parents if I could apply for my junior year. They told me if I got accepted, they would find the funds to pay my tuition, room, and board. Lo and behold, I got accepted! Truth be known, the Universitas per Stranieri accepted everyone, but we didn't know that, and plans were put in place for me to leave on a student ship on June 7, 1966.

There's a country and western song by Thomas Rhett with lyrics that say, "You make your plans and hear God laughing." That's the way this adventure started. First of all, getting seven children, who comprised four teenagers including myself, to agree on a road trip was a challenge. Right before the trip, one brother fell out of a tree and broke his arm, and one brother got a summer job and refused to leave. As a result, my parents rethought the whole idea of the family taking a road trip to New York. So, it was decided that I would take an overnight train from Chicago to New York City, then a cab to the boat. The family did accompany me to the train station in Chicago where there was much hugging, kissing, and crying. At the last moment, my father gave me a sealed card, which I have treasured all these years, with instructions to open it after the train got under way.

I have every card and letter my father has ever sent me as they number less than 10. They are all special for this reason.

As I opened this card, expecting fatherly words of wisdom, the card said, "So, you're going to Europe... BIG DEAL... I was born there!!"

I loved and still love Europe. Gerry and I have visited many times and have taken our children several times. In fact, our daughter has been living and working in the Bavarian Alps for many years and to date has visited 65 countries. Believe it or not, there is an app to track that! Our son was privileged to attend the Model UN High School Conference in Paris at 18, where he called us from the terrace of the Paris Four Seasons Hotel and informed us that he was having a whiskey sour and smoking a Cuban cigar, which caused my husband to comment that he wished he had his son's life!

But I digress. I really intended to study Italian the year I was in Europe and visit as many places as I could on vacations. But on November 4, 1966, I learned a new term in Italian, "il diluvio (the flood)." It was a worse flood than the 1557 flood during Michelangelo's time. Today, the only traces of the devastation are two marks on the wall of a building in the corner of the Piazza Santa Croce, one for the flood of 1557 and the other a little higher for the flood of 1966. Everything in Florence came to a standstill. Everything except for me. It was the perfect excuse for me to leave Florence and explore the world.

After spending Christmas and New Year's in Germany, I returned to Italy, moved to Rome, and still my wanderlust prevailed. I decided to go to Asia. A friend of mine gave me an inexpensive alternative to taking the train. Her dressmaker was going to Naples to visit his family and would give me a ride if I split the gas with him. So, I purchased a ticket from Naples to Istanbul on a freighter, and off we went.

Halfway to Naples, it started raining extremely hard. The small 500 Fiat slid on the autostrada (highway). When my driving companion stepped on the brakes to stop the car from sliding, the car flipped on its side. Fortunately, we were able to get out through the roof. We called the Italian equivalent of AAA and after the car was righted, I opted to return to Rome and chalk the trip up to a bad experience. The next morning, I called the travel agency to see if I could get a refund on my ticket and rebook another freighter; however, I was told the boat had been held up and would leave at midnight that evening.

I bought the train ticket, which cost more money than driving. But considering the train stayed on its rails the whole way to Naples, it was a bargain. I got to the boat in time to sail with it.

To save money, I decided to get a ticket with what is called "senza vita," which means "without life" or "without food." It was a calculated thing. I was getting on the boat at midnight where I intended to go to sleep. The ship was making a port of call in Piraeus, Greece, in the morning, where it would stay for six hours taking on passengers, at which time I could get off and buy something to eat. From there, it would take off for Istanbul, arriving early morning the next day. I certainly wouldn't starve in those 36 hours.

***

Gerald Alois Harles was the first white baby born in an Inuit hospital to Czechoslovakian parents in Pouce Coupe, Canada. His mother refused to acknowledge him when he was brought to her at first, because he was born with black hair, rather than the blond hair she was expecting, and she was sure he was switched with an Inuit baby. The story goes, his father convinced her otherwise and by the time he was two, he had the white, blond hair she thought he should have had at birth.

Gerry's parents had left Czechoslovakia, or Sudetenland as Hitler called it, in 1938. His mother traveled by train, on a forged British passport as a British nanny returning to England, and his father on a motorcycle with the help of the British Underground. His father was one of the leaders of the Social Democratic Party, which was anti-Nazi, and as such, was an enemy of the Third Reich. They were married in Westminster Abbey and given a choice of being sent to Australia or Canada. They chose Canada, figuring it would be easier to get back to Europe after the war.

Unfortunately, this urban couple, along with approximately 1,000 other Sudetens, were sent to the frozen Canadian north to homestead in Tomslake, Pouce Coupe, Canada, which is mile 0 on the ALCAN Highway. Gerry's father was an accountant and his mother a seamstress. His father was resentful of life's circumstances and the need to learn agricultural skills in his late 30s. His mother never did assimilate to country life.

Although both parents were hard workers and did achieve success in their new life, their dream was to get back to Europe, their family, and the way of life they had left behind. This was compounded by the fact that when Gerry's paternal grandparents came for a visit, the Czechoslovakian government immediately declared them "persona non grata" and seized all their property and bank accounts in Prague. When the Canadian government denied them Canadian citizenship based on their ages, the negotiated solution was a stateless passport reflecting the fact that they were without a country. A hard pill to swallow for a couple who had lived their whole married lives in the same home, in the same town, Prague, Czechoslovakia.

As with all children growing up on farms far from big cities, maturity comes early. Riding horses, driving tractors, shooting guns, common survival instincts were a necessity, and Gerry was a fast learner, unlike his urbane parents. He was a precocious child, a handful for his parents. When he was four years old, they sent him to school. That first evening when he returned home, there was a note pinned to his shirt that said in effect that although he was mentally ready for school, the teacher was not mentally ready for him. The note explained that in as much as he was too young for school anyway, it would be appreciated if they would keep him at home until the school had to take him.

When Gerry was able to attend school, he was a difficult student. Some 'adventures' included a reenactment of the story of William Tell's apple incident (this from Alice, the girl who had the apple on her head and arrow in her forehead), and the story of running Alice's underpants up the flagpole (Alice, believe it or not, is still a good friend; someday I would like to read her story), to list some of the more benign incidents.

When he was young, Gerry satisfied the wanderlust in his veins by running away from home. It was not that he had an unhappy home life, it was his DNA. His father always found him and brought him home. That was until the summer when he got a job selling tickets to the ole swimming hole. (This was a legitimate job. I have pictures.) He saved up his earnings and hitch-hiked to Edmonton and bought a car. It was the first car the family owned. I would like to think his parents were proud of him as he was only 14 years old!

When Gerry was 15 years old, he got a summer job on the pipeline, which was being built from Canada to Alaska. He worked in the laundry, cleaned out the gambling trailer, and served the meals. He was hired as a server, but the laundry and gambling trailer provided extra money. How does a 15-year-old run a laundry? "Simple," he told me. Once a week, he and another young man collected all the dirty clothes, threw them in a large pot filled with hot water and laundry detergent, and stirred the whole thing around. Then they would take the clothes and put them in a pot of clean water to rinse them, take them out, and hang them along the fence that surrounded the living area of the camp. When the men came in from the pipeline, they would pick out their clothes and take them to their trailers.

As for cleaning out the gambling trailer, when the men were paid twice a month, the gambling trailer was opened. Gerry said some men would gamble away their whole pay in one night. In the morning when he went in to clean out the trailer, he would find money all over the floor. He was told he could keep whatever he found. For that reason, Gerry would never gamble, except one time in Las Vegas when he won $800 from a slot machine at The Venetian that 'whispered to him' as he got off the elevator, and another time in the Republic of Panama when he took a hit on 16 and above eight times in a row scoring 21 with two different dealers... but those are stories for another time.

One of Gerry's most important jobs from a learning experience was that of a gas station attendant. It was not the job itself that was so significant, but the man he worked for, Keith Fisher-Fleming, who became his first mentor. Keith was a veteran of the Burmese War where he had lost one of his legs. He and his wife owned the gas station, which was on mile 1 of the ALCAN Highway. Gerry told Keith about his dream of leaving Tomslake and traveling the world. Keith spoke to Gerry about his dream of going to law school and being appointed the Governor of Hong Kong. Keith told Gerry he intended to achieve his dream, and all Gerry had to do to achieve his was to stay positive and work towards making it happen.

When Gerry was 17 years old, his parents sold everything they owned in Canada and moved back to Europe, settling in Fürth, Germany, where the majority of the Harles clan had settled after the war. Thus began a series of nondescript jobs that Gerry bounced between learning various trades as well as the German language. His most significant job was for a contractor rebuilding the road system that was damaged during the war. But most importantly, it was another opportunity to earn extra money. At night, Gerry would use the contractor's backhoe to dig out various farmers' cesspools, which was very lucrative until he got the machine stuck in one of the holes one night! Banned to a stretch of road where his job was to go back and forth in first gear, leveling the roadbed, Gerry decided that he had to change his circumstances. Keith Fisher Fleming had told him to stay positive and work towards making his dream an actuality. What to do? Till the end of his life, Gerry did not know from where it came. But one night after he had made the decision to change his circumstances, he had a dream to become a car salesman. The next morning, dressed in work boots, denim trousers, a flannel shirt, and a leather jacket, he went to the office of the sales manager of Mercedes Benz and asked for a job. He was turned down. Ever optimistic, he made the rounds of every car dealership in Nuremberg until he was given a chance for a junior sales position at Volkswagen.

He worked himself up from junior salesman to full-fledged salesman. Because of his fluency in English, he was given the US military market. Now, there was a hitch in the car sales market in Germany in 1963–1964. The waiting time from deposit to delivery of a car was six months. That was the bad news. The good news was the fact that with a $50 deposit, when the automobile was ready for delivery, the contract could be transferred to anybody. So, Gerry started writing contracts with $50 deposits. In six months, he was the only salesman who could immediately deliver a car. Anyone could have done this, but not anyone could sell cars like Gerry, who went from junior salesman to top salesman in only a year!

In 1966, Gerry took an extended ski vacation, and when he returned to Germany, the folks at Volkswagen were not happy at his lengthy absence and decided to renegotiate his commission. This was not acceptable to Gerry. He had recently been approached by American Motors and offered the military market in the Middle East to include Turkey, Syria, Iraq, Iran, and Lebanon. So, thanking Volkswagen for giving him his first job in sales, he said farewell and moved on to American Motors. Volkswagen's reply was "you'll be back."

Well, he never did go back. In March 1967, he loaded his 1967 American Motors DPL Sedan on a freighter and embarked on his second trip to Turkey.

***

Everything went according to plan. In Piraeus, I got off the ship, took public transportation into Athens, and saw the Acropolis. I then walked through the historical streets, bought some candy and fruit, ate a sandwich, and made it back before the gangplank was pulled up. I went to the bar, which is the social hub of any boat and a good place to meet one's fellow passengers. I was immediately struck by one very obnoxious individual. He was sitting with his back to the bar, both elbows on the bar, surveying the rest of the passengers. He had on a red turtleneck sweater, was drinking a scotch on the rocks, and was smoking a very fat cigar.

I sat down at the bar and struck up a conversation with a Turkish doctor, who was returning home after spending eight years in the United States at an American hospital, and an American engineer on his way to a Department of Defense assignment. I was definitely out of my league, but it didn't help that Mr. Obnoxious disagreed with everything I said. And what, I wondered, was Mr. Obnoxious's story? What was he doing at this time, in this place, on this boat?

I cannot even remember what the conversation was about but as I said, Gerry disagreed with everything I was saying. It was me and the Turkish doctor against Gerry and the engineer, who pretty much agreed with Gerry. We were about to get heated over whatever it was we were discussing when the dinner bell sounded, and everyone got up to go to the dining room. Gerry asked me why I wasn't coming, and I told him I had taken a "senza vita" passage but not to worry, I had eaten in Piraeus.

During his dinner, the man I referred to as Mr. Obnoxious made a sandwich with the bread from the breadbasket and the cheese from the dessert tray, wrapped it in his napkin, and gave it to me at the bar, so "I wouldn't starve." We spent the rest of the night getting to know each other. He told me he was a 45-year-old businessman. That wasn't true, which I found out later when I saw his passport. He was 25. He said he was on his way to US bases in Turkey to sell US servicemen Ramblers. I shared I was a 20-year-old college student doing a year abroad. I told him about losing my university in the flood in Florence and my goal of seeing as much of the Middle East and Southeast Asia as possible. With that goal in mind, I asked him if I could tag along with him as he traveled from base to base. I had heard that Turkey was a great place to visit ancient historical sites. I promised him that as soon as we got close to the border of Iran, we would part ways as my original goal was to make my way to India, a country which, unfortunately, I have never seen to this day.

We talked until the bar closed and then gallantly, Gerry walked me down to the lowest deck where I had a berth in the dormitory with 24 other women. I fell asleep anticipating my adventures in Turkey. Gerry fell asleep listening to the throbbing of the engines for although he had a first-class cabin, he couldn't find his way out of the lower deck. He blamed it on the design of the freighter; personally, I think it was the Johnnie Walker.

THE TAG-ALONG—TURKEY

Arriving in Istanbul, Gerry and I split up for customs. I had my one suitcase, and Gerry had his car filled with brochures and his suitcase filled with suits, so he told me to wait for him on the other side. About a half an hour later, as I was waiting in line for my turn, Gerry came up to me and asked me what was taking so long. Well, to be fair, I was behind the Turkish doctor, who, with his wife, probably had a trunk for every year they were in the United States. Gerry simply smiled at the customs official, handed him something, and suddenly, I was through customs.

The next order of business was checking into a hotel. Gerry drove straight to the Istanbul Hilton and was amazed when I told him I had no intention of checking in along with him as the Hilton was about 15 times more expensive than I was willing to spend. So, after he got himself checked in, we spent the next two hours going from pensione to pensione until we found one I could afford.

Poor Gerry, this was just a precursor to the experience he was going to have the next day helping me cash the $100 check my parents had sent me for the month of March. Not only did I want more than the legal rate of 9 to 1, which I had heard was possible in Turkey, but I only wanted to cash $10 in Turkish lira and the rest in US dollars, something that would have been easier if the amount had been far larger!

Gerry finally put me in a taxi, gave the driver some money, and told him to take me to the bank. He had to go to work.

The rest of the week, Gerry worked, and I visited all the historical sites in Istanbul: Hagia Sofia, the oldest Christian church in Istanbul, turned into a mosque and then a museum; the Topkapi Palace Museum, the palace of the Ottoman sultans, where Jacqueline Kennedy had tea as the First Lady under a magnificent 41/2-ton Czechoslovakian crystal chandelier; the Blue Mosque; and many other wondrous sights, not to mention sampling the Turkish vanilla cookies and pudding. On Saturday, Gerry took a day off, and we revisited all the highlights previously mentioned along with the sunken cisterns built by the Romans and still used in 1967. I understand in the 2000s it is also used as a concert hall. We also spent two-and-a-half hours in the covered bazaar, or Kapalilarsi, that I had discovered the day before. The objective on this day was to buy a leather coat for Gerry and a pair of earrings for my sister. I realized Gerry was a tireless, ball-breaking shopper. In other words, he was like a dog with a bone when he gets something he wants. He will not let go until it is his. I chose the earrings in ten minutes. Two hours later, Gerry got his leather coat.

Early the next morning, we got up and got ready to leave Istanbul, cross the Bosporus, and officially enter Asia. The boat afforded a breathtaking view of the Bosporus and then we were on our way to Ankara. The trip was certainly eye opening if not relaxing. The countryside was beautiful in a rough sort of way. There weren't many trees but green fields, mountains, and lakes were plentiful. Also plentiful was traffic; cars, driving on the wrong side of the road, buses loaded with people inside and baggage on top, going 80 mph passing you; little kids throwing stones at your car, even one man aiming a shotgun at us. On the plus side, we did have lunch on top of a mountain—good food with a lovely view. I was relieved to reach our destination. Gerry did not seem a bit fazed at the whole scene. In fact, he seemed to enjoy my discomfort!

We stayed in Ankara for over a week. I went from one tourist attraction to another and Gerry sold cars. If the truth be known, in 1967, there was not that much to see in Ankara, so I would sleep late and spend the afternoons exploring. Sometimes, I would go with Gerry to the base and have a good ole American hamburger.

One night, we were invited for drinks atop the Ankara Hilton by George, the owner of the hotel where we were staying. Gerry was thinking of going into business with him, importing cars into Lebanon, his native country. George was a true gentleman; unfortunately, he had a very obnoxious son by the name of Sammy.

While George and Gerry were talking about the feasibility of this business venture, Sammy asked me to dance. I accepted to be polite, plus I do like to dance. After a couple of dances, I could see that George was leaving, so I thanked Sammy and went back over to our table. When Sammy got a little possessive, I told Gerry we should go. He agreed, and we went down to the lobby. Gerry left me in the lobby and went to get the car. When he came back to get me, Sammy and his friends had locked the lobby doors.

I asked the front desk to unlock the doors, and they just laughed. Gerry yelled through the glass for me to get behind the concierge desk, which I did. He rammed the doors with the car. I ran to the car, he put it in reverse, and we left. That was the last time we visited that Hilton.

That night, as we were having probably one too many night caps at our hotel bar, Gerry asked me to marry him. A little shocked, but not wanting to close that door, I told him I would think about it.

A few days later, after a few too many night caps again at our hotel bar, I brought up the marriage subject and asked, "Remember when you were drunk the other night and asked me to marry you, and I said I would think about it? Well, I'm drunk now, so yes, I'll marry you."

He looked at me and said, "Judy, I was not drunk."

I replied, "Neither am I."

After 10 days in Ankara, we took off for the Black Sea and two bases situated there, Sinope and Samsum. Sinope must have been a base that had something to do with computers. I know that the year was 1967, but the men had a song they sung with verses that were very funny. They were all about some piece of equipment that was always breaking.

My thoughts in hindsight were it was a monitoring system that kept track of whatever was across from Sinope—due east is Russia... just sayin'. Sinope also had a radio station that at two in the morning was more than happy to let Gerry 'spin the discs' and comment on the songs.

The road to Sinope was barren and dry. We took a seven-and-a-half-hour trip from Ankara to the Black Sea through the interior of Turkey. The road from Sinope to Samsum was spectacular, fertile, and green. The road ran along the mountains and was very narrow. It would have been a beautiful drive if Gerry had not decided to take it at 80 mph.

One of the more interesting facts I observed along the way was the large number of blond-haired, blue-eyed people in a country where most of the people had dark eyes and dark hair. Gerry speculated that they were probably Kurds, as there was a large colony of Kurds to the southeast of Samsum.

Samsum itself was an interesting experience. I can't even remember if Gerry managed to sell any cars, but that night in the NCO Club, we were the center of an 'incident.' It involved a lot of liquor and talk of where we would like to live. Gerry started the conversation in German with the German wife of the cook saying he would like to live somewhere in North America, and Max, the top sergeant I had been speaking to, butted in and asked, "Why not Italy?" to which Gerry replied that, in his opinion, Italy was 75% communist. Max took offense and threw Gerry off his chair and Gerry managed to clear the table of glasses getting himself up. Well, the 'incident' was beginning to look more and more like a bar fight and the MPs were called and we were asked to leave.

The next day, Gerry was refused entrance to the base for being a communist sympathizer. Fortunately, Gerry had a friend on the base who investigated the 'incident' and found out the whole matter was orchestrated by Max, who was upset when I rebuffed his advances! I can't even remember the man or the advance!

At any rate, the charge of being communist sympathizers was expunged from our records and we were free to visit other bases.

We returned to Ankara for a day, then took off for Adana. Turkey in 1967, a huge country, the interior of which was underdeveloped, lacked decent hotels along the way. So, it was necessary to plan one's trip for eight hours at a time. As it was, when we got to Adana, all we would find was literally a flea bag hotel that first night. The second night, we checked into the best hotel in town, the Agba Hotel, which was only just a bit better. Gerry had a long talk with the concierge about his car, threatening him with all sorts of dire things if anything happened to it. The next morning, when he came out to go to the base, he noticed his hubcaps were missing. He yelled for the concierge just about the time the man came out of the hotel carrying his hubcaps. The man had locked them in the safe for the night 'just to be safe!'

I decided to join Gerry on the base since there was little 'tourist wise' to see in Adana. Gerry told me where to go to catch the military bus to the base. As I was waiting for the bus, which was on a bridge over a ravine, a bunch of men in the ravine started throwing stones at me. Unwisely, I picked up some of the stones and threw them back.

Then some beggars approached me for a handout. Truth be told, all I had on me was a $20 bill. I did not have any lira, and I told them I couldn't help them. This angered them and they shouted down to the men below who were throwing stones. I was being surrounded by a mob of unfriendly Turkish men and wondering how I was going to extricate myself when the bus arrived. I have never been so thankful to see a bus before or since!

We spent Easter in Adana. Gerry, always thinking about how to best sell cars, hit on the idea of approaching the ministers on base and offering them a bonus in the plate if they announce that he was on base selling cars. The deal was, for every car sold on Easter Sunday, he would give the Church $25.00. It was a successful plan; Gerry sold 25 cars and gave the Church $625.00. Unfortunately, not all those cars were delivered, thanks to American Motors closing their factory early, but that's what propelled Gerry to Asia three months later.

From Adana, it was back to Ankara to regroup and head off to Izmir. On the way, there is a small base called Site 23. As we passed the bus stop outside the base, Gerry spied a guy with a suitcase. This was a sure sign to Gerry that the man was getting ready to go home. So, I hopped in the back seat and the man sat in front. Gerry dropped him off at his house and made an appointment for later that evening to sell him a car. He then dropped me off at a friend of his where we were going to spend the night before leaving for Izmir.

Gerry went back to the man's house and was successful in selling him a car. There was another man there who was also going home and was impressed with Gerry's sales pitch and decided to purchase a car as well. Gerry went out to his car to get another sales contract, which he kept in his center console. As he went to unlock his car, he realized that it was already unlocked, but that fact didn't register immediately. He slid into the driver's seat, got the contract out of the center console, and as he got ready to leave the car, he saw a man with an ice pick behind him in the rear-view mirror. He grabbed the man's head and managed to wrestle him out of the car. He dragged him to the door of the customer who had just bought the car and shouted for him to call the police.

The customer, who was in the US military, told him that if he got involved, they would 'flag' his records and hold up his rotation date, but there was an MP station down the street. So, Gerry dragged the thief down the street to the MP station. The MPs started filling out their forms but when they found out Gerry was Canadian, they told him they couldn't help him. They told him that he needed to call the Turkish police, which they did for him. The Turkish police came and arrested the thief… and Gerry. Gerry's appointment was at 7pm. We didn't hear from him until seven the next morning!

When he arrived at his friends' home, he insisted that we leave for Izmir immediately. He was shaken and obviously in need of sleep. He said the Turkish police wanted something from the thief and made him watch while they tortured him. He thought that they let him go when the thief died. As much as he could make out, it had something to do with a plot against the government and fancy cars. I convinced him to get a few hours' sleep and then we would take off.

We took off for Izmir at noon, a few miles outside of the outskirts of Ankara. We were almost run off the road by a caravan of luxury cars, all flying various national flags, speeding towards Ankara. We found out the next day that the caravan was apprehended by a joint force of Turkish police and military forces. According to the paper, the caravan was filled with rebels attempting to overthrow the Turkish government. We figured that Gerry's car was supposed to be in that caravan but was thwarted by a Canadian attempting to sell a car to a GI!

On our way to Izmir, we intended to stop at a base in Eskisehir. Gerry had never stopped at that base before, but I told him my roommate in Rome had a cousin stationed on the base, so I was familiar with the fact that it existed. Well, it was a little out of our way, but Gerry said if he could sell a few cars, it would be worth the trip. After a few more hours than we figured, we finally arrived at the base. The first thing we noticed was the fact that the gate guards were Turkish MPs—not a good sign for an American base. We optimistically plugged on and talked our way onto the base, asking for my friend's cousin, who was no longer on the base, but we did speak with one of the GIs stationed there who told us that there were only nine US soldiers on the base as advisors and none of them were short enough to want to buy a car. I guess that was why my friend's cousin kept saying in his letters that he was so lonely! The experience did not make any points for me with Gerry.

Since we were now a good five hours further from Izmir, we were running out of gas, so we began looking for a gas station. When we found one, we realized we did not have any Turkish lira, but everyone takes US dollars, right? Well, not in 1967 in central Turkey. The first gas station flat turned us down.

The second gas station turned us down as well, but there was a bus full of passengers there, so everyone got out and examined the $20 bill along with my receipt from the Turkish American Bank, where I had cashed twenty dollars that first day in Istanbul, which showed the exchange rate. Well, after everyone turned the $20 bill every which way and looked at the receipt upside down, we concluded it was a lost cause. I then told Gerry, "Let's go down the road, and at the next station, just have the guy 'fill it up' and then give him the money." Gerry thought that was a great idea, which made up for the Eskisehir idea, so off we went.

At the next station, everything went according to plan until Gerry gave the man the $20 bill. There was a lot of yelling in Turkish. Soon, a young boy came out with a pail and a hose and not only siphoned out the gas that the station put in but what little we had left as well! Next to the station was an 18-wheeler on its way to Europe. Fortunately, the driver spoke a little German, and knew what a $20 bill was. He told Gerry he could exchange it for Turkish lira. He asked Gerry what the exchange rate was (I got 9 lira to $1 at the bank, but you could get more on the black market) and Gerry told him, "12 to 1."

The man laughed and said he would give him 6 to 1.

Gerry said, "But I can get 9 to 1 at the bank."

The driver laughed again and said, "Do I look like the bank?"

He had a point. Gerry took 6 to 1, shook his hand, and we got our gas. Of course, we had to also pay for the gas we already had in our tank! Before leaving the station, we then had to sit down with the station manager and have a cup of chai, which is hot, sweet tea. A Turkish custom which indicates that there are no hard feelings after a negotiation. Not a bad custom when you think about it, and the tea is delicious.

We again started for Izmir, Gerry driving as fast as the potholed road permitted as it was getting dark, and except for the occasional small village, the road was without any kind of light. To add insult to injury, it began to rain, and just as I was thinking it couldn't get much worse, we hit a stone and blew out our right front tire. Gerry turned to me and asked, "Have you ever changed a tire, because I never have?"

I thought back to the winter of 1958/59 when my dad broke his leg, and my mom was pregnant, and one by one, all the tires on our only car went flat. My brother and I changed them one by one. So, yes, I did know how to change a tire. But in the rain? In Turkey?

I said, "Well, I did know how ten years ago, but I think I would be more helpful if I held my raincoat in front of the headlight to give you some light and give you pointers along the way." And that's what we did, and Gerry changed a tire for the first and last time in his life!! Nine eventful hours from the time we left Ankara, we rolled into Izmir, checked into our hotel, showered, and celebrated our arrival with a nice dinner.

Izmir is a beautiful town, a stark contrast to the other towns in Asian Turkey we had visited. Formerly called Smyrna, it is one of the oldest cities on the Mediterranean. With over 8,500 years of civilization, ruled in turn by the Persians, the Romans, and the Ottoman Empire, it thrilled my tourist heart to no end with all the places to visit while Gerry set up shop at the commissary to sell cars. My first foray into touring was to go to Kadifekale Castle, built during the reign of Alexander the Great by one of his generals. The trip was arduous, through depressed neighborhoods, and sometimes a little scary, but I must admit, the result was a spectacular view of Izmir.

Easier to reach was Konak Square, a gathering place, for it seemed everyone in Izmir. I made a mental note to bring Gerry back to see the Yali Mosque and the Clock Tower, both amazing works of art. When I got back to the hotel, Gerry was already there. He told me he had met a very nice stockbroker and had made a date with him and his girlfriend to have dinner with us that evening. But first, he had to change some US dollars into Turkish lira. He said he would be back before the couple arrived. But just in case, the guy's name was David, and they would meet us in the bar at 7:30pm.

At 7:30, Gerry was not back and about 10 minutes later, the room phone rang and David said they were at the bar. I said Gerry was on an errand, but I would be right down. Well, for the next hour, I got to know David and his girlfriend while we speculated why it would take Gerry so long to change money, since he had left around six that evening. At about 8:45, Gerry came into the bar, his tie all wrinkled, his shirt with the buttons torn off, and all covered in blood. Seemed Gerry went looking for the elusive 12 to 1 exchange rate, which rumor had, it was at the Russian Embassy.

Two men picked him up at the hotel and took him to a house, where he gave one of the men $100 while the other man waited with Gerry. Five minutes later, the first man ran out of the house yelling, "Go! Go! The police are here."

He jumped into the car and told Gerry he had lost his money. At which time, Gerry grabbed the driver and threatened to choke him to death unless the first man gave him back his $100. The first man then grabbed Gerry and threatened to kill him unless he let go of the driver. All of this was happening as the driver was driving. This went on for about 45 minutes until, finally, the first man gave Gerry 700 lira for his $100, or 200 liras less than he would have received had he gone to the bank.

Gerry then took a taxi back to the hotel. On the bright side, it was 100 lira more than the trucker gave him the day before on our way to Izmir. No chai was consumed with this transaction! Gerry washed up, changed his shirt and tie, and we went out for dinner, deciding that someday we would laugh about this.

Izmir was the highlight of our trip. Not only was it culturally the capital of Turkey, but we had met a lifelong friend to 'play' with. Every weekend, we went some place different, exploring the ancient ruins, like Ephesus, the site of the Temple of Artemis, one of the seven wonders of the ancient world; Pergamon, the cultural capital of Ancient Greece; and *Çeşme*, where we swam in the Aegean Sea and in a natural hot spring. Our new friend, David, and Gerry had one annoying thing in common. Gerry loved to drive extremely fast, and David delighted in encouraging him to go faster.

One Sunday, the boys decided it would be fun to go rabbit hunting. They drove up the coast where they rented a boat with a captain, and we motored out to an island that had rabbits. Well, the captain did not believe in hunting. David's girlfriend knew how to cook rabbits but did not know how to skin them. I figured I could probably skin them thanks to biology class but did not have the stomach for it.

So, we had a quick meeting and decided the best thing for all concerned was to bury them. We did such a good job that when all was said and done, we convinced Gerry and David that they missed all the rabbits and they just hopped off. We then motored back to the mainland and had a great lunch before going back to Izmir.

The week before Gerry's 26th birthday, he left for Karamursel AFB, which was the last base he intended to visit in Turkey. I did not go with him as I had bought some material in the bazaar and had ordered two dresses and a suit to be made by a local tailor as fast as possible, which necessitated several fittings that week. But by the weekend, several of us decided to go to Istanbul, picking up Gerry along the way, and helped him celebrate his birthday.

We took off early Friday and got to the base around 2pm, only to find that we must have passed Gerry going back to Izmir somewhere along the way. I wanted to turn around and return to Izmir, but I was overruled, and we continued to Istanbul, where I spent a miserable weekend wishing I were back in Izmir.

The trip back was a nightmare. It was deja vu all over again, as we blew a tire, but this time we did not have a spare, so we had to find a garage at nine o'clock on Sunday evening and someone who could patch a tire! To make matters worse, we were in the Turkish countryside among people who were not used to seeing American girls in miniskirts. Fortunately, the guys gave us their long raincoats. We finally limped into Izmir at one in the morning. A very angry Gerry was waiting for me. He told me he had decided to leave for Athens the next morning. Angrier words ensued, and we finally decided to get some rest and hash it out in the morning.

Morning came and Gerry was steadfast in his resolve to leave Turkey immediately. I had to stay until the clothes I had ordered were finished. So, he left, and I stayed. His one concession was if I cabled my flight arrangements, he would meet my plane. Gerry then drove to Çeşme and found someone on a ferry boat large enough to carry his car across the Aegean Sea to Greece. This was no mean feat since, on April 21, 1967, the Greek government was taken over by a military junta.

A week later, I joined Gerry in Greece in his apartment in Glyfada. After seeing a bit of Athens, sampling lots of Greek seafood, and dreaming of the luxurious life from Gerry's balcony, which overlooked a marina on the Mediterranean Sea, I decided I'd better return to Italy, retrieve my trunk and everything I had stored with American Express, and close out my life in Florence. So, back I went "senza vita" on the ferry to Naples, then by train to Florence.

Unfortunately, American Express's storage facility was damaged by the flood. Most of my things were not salvageable. I saved what I could and threw out what was ruined. My biggest disappointment was the loss of all my pictures. Fortunately, the Latin books I borrowed from the University of Illinois were able to be dried out. I purchased a trunk in the market and shipped everything I had salvaged back to the States, then returned to Athens.

Saying goodbye to Italy made me sad. Yes, I was ready to leave and start a new chapter in my life, but in a way, a part of me would always belong there. It's like a poem I read once where you long for a place you've never been and then you go, and you immediately feel like you belong. But enough of the maudlin thoughts.

On the boat, I ran into John, the Rosenthal salesman. John was a friend of Gerry's who we had met along the way in Turkey selling china the same way Gerry was selling cars. John was now returning to Istanbul with his wife to attend a Rosenthal convention. I invited John and his wife to join Gerry and me at the Athens NCO Club for lunch, when the boat docked in the six-hour layover, which they accepted.

We were all having a good time when John turned to Gerry and asked him what his plans were. I took the question to mean what Gerry and my plans were. Gerry answered that he was thinking of going to Japan to sell cars. He was disillusioned with American Motors. They had closed their factory early, and he was getting daily cables telling him he had to contact such-and-such a customer and get them to change their order or it would be cancelled. They had no concept of how big Turkey was and how far apart the bases were. Not to mention that most of his customers were already in the United States.

All my plans seemed to be going up in smoke. Here I was all ready to get married. I even had a sexy white mini dress with a matching coat made in Izmir. My mother had—I found out later—decided to go to Athens. And Gerry's idea of the future was to go to Japan and sell cars.

When we got back to the apartment, our discussion heated up. Words flew back and forth, and I finally threw out the thought that if I hadn't met him, I would be finishing college. Gerry's reply was, "Well,

24

finish college and then look me up." He then proceeded to go out on the balcony and sunbathe.

I resorted to reading the Stars and Stripes, where the headline stated that the Vietnam War was getting so sophisticated that there were car salesmen on the DMZ. Further along in the paper there was an advertisement for car salesmen. I took the paper out to the balcony, draped it over Gerry's head and said those historic words, "Well, if you insist on going to Asia, you might as well get into a war while you're at it."

Gerry sat up and started going through the paper until he came to the ad for a car salesman in Vietnam. He got excited when he read the ad, claiming he knew who put the ad in the paper. He told me if it was who he thought it was, the position was for selling Dodge, Chrysler, and Plymouth cars. He immediately called the number in the ad and made an appointment to meet with an Arnold Weber in Frankfurt one week later.

I toyed with the idea of staying in Greece, or even going back to Italy and getting a job, but homesickness and the fact that Gerry would not be with me won over and I called my parents asking them to send me money for the price of the airfare home.

Within 24 hours of making the decision to leave Greece, Gerry had notified his landlady of his decision to leave, closed out all his utility accounts, while I packed his things to go to Germany and my things to return to the States. We took off for Nurnberg, driving 36 hours straight, stopping only for three hours' rest by the side of the road.

We drove around Albania, whose borders were closed to Americans in 1967, then straight through Yugoslavia, which today would have covered North Macedonia, Kosovo, Montenegro, Serbia, Bosnia and Herzegovina, Croatia, and Slovenia! I do not kid when I say I have been to countries the names of which I do not know! The road through Austria crossed the Alps at 8,000 feet, which could have been spectacular with 10-foot snow drifts if it hadn't been so foggy that we couldn't see the end of the car. We finally arrived in Nurnberg at 8am. Gerry took me to a hotel in town and went home to see his mother, who he hadn't seen since moving to Greece.

I saw very little of Gerry in the next couple of days as he was saying goodbye to his friends, interviewing for the job in Vietnam, and getting ready to leave Germany for what was to be at least a year. Meanwhile, I picked up the money my parents had wired me, mailed two boxes of clothes and miscellaneous items to my parents, purchased a ticket on Air Icelandic from Frankfurt to New York, and out of desperation, took a trolly to Gerry's mother's house to meet her. I figured, if he wasn't going to introduce me, I would introduce myself.

My pushiness paid off. Mrs. Harles was a truly charming woman, and we got along wonderfully. She was impressed with the way I had packed Gerry's clothes. Apparently, he'd have just thrown his clothes in the suitcase. I was impressed with her cooking, and her knowledge of opera and travel. Her life story was amazing. Her hobbies were traveling, skiing, and swimming. She liked the idea that I was from a large family. She equated that with stability. In short, I had his mother in my corner, and she stayed there all the years Gerry and I were married!

The day before we left for Frankfurt, the hotel where I was staying told me I had to move out. I told them I was leaving the next morning. The manager told me no, I had to leave that morning. I told him that wasn't the deal. I had no idea what the deal was. Gerry had checked me in and negotiated the nightly price in German, but I had no intention of looking for a hotel for one night. Especially when I had no real way of letting Gerry know where I was, short of taking the trolley to his house and telling his mother. Well, that afternoon, as I was laying out the outfit I was going to wear on the trip the next day, I was missing my blouse and scarf. I went down to the lobby and reported to the concierge that the items were missing and suggested that perhaps the maid had 'misplaced' them. They assured me this did not happen. I innocently thought that perhaps I had mistakenly put them in one of the two boxes I had mailed to my parents from American Express and chose another blouse and scarf for the trip.

That night, about midnight, I left my room to use the washroom, which was in the hall. After I got back to my room, I locked myself in and went to sleep. A few hours later, I was awakened by a soft knock on the door. I went to the door and asked who it was, thinking it might have been Gerry. The answer was the police. The voice said I should open the door; it was about my blouse. Now, my door locked with two clicks. The first click would lock it, but the second click was like a dead bolt.

I remembered that I had only locked it once when I came back from the washroom, but I couldn't remember which way the key turned to double click it. I closed my eyes, said a prayer, and turned the key to the right. I heard a click a second before the door handle turned. I had guessed right; the door was double locked, and I did not intend to open it. Whoever was on the other side became frustrated and started beating on the door. I ran to the window and yelled for the polizei at the top of my lungs. I then locked the shutter on the window and had a very bad rest of the night. Gerry picked me up in the morning; he settled the bill for me, getting me a further discount for my awful night! As far as I was concerned, I couldn't get out of Germany fast enough.

In Frankfurt, we said goodbye. I was headed back home to Lake Forest, Illinois, to finish college, and Gerry was headed to Saigon (Ho Chi Minh City), Vietnam. We promised each other that as soon as I finished my education, I would join Gerry wherever he was, most likely in Vietnam. We promised undying love for each other, then we said goodbye.

BACK IN
THE UNITED STATES

While Gerry was herding a dozen or so unruly salesmen to Vietnam, who were treating the experience as a vacation and/or an adventure, I was back in the good ole United States trying to figure out how I could finish 60 hours of college credits in the fastest way possible. At first, I thought I could skip the whole college thing entirely and get a job as a stewardess flying with one of the airlines that circled the globe. But as my father pointed out, qualifying for that job would take almost as long as finishing those remaining 60 hours; besides, learning how to be a server 30,000 feet in the air was not exactly the career I had in mind. So, at my father's insistence, I picked up the University of Illinois course catalog, which was about 300 pages thick, and plotted out 60 hours of courses that would correspond to living in Asia for the next few years.

I spent the summer working at Great Lakes Naval Training Center at an NCO Club as a server. Come September, Dad and I went back to the University of Illinois (U of I) to convince the Dean of Housing that although I was not yet 21, the rule for independent housing, my last year of traveling in Europe should qualify me to live in independent housing. The good news was that the dean agreed and signed off on the permission slip. The bad news was that now I had to find a place to live. By November, and three apartments later, I finally found a suitable place, close to campus with my own room, and roommates I liked.

Of all the subjects I took, the ones that interested me the most were those on India. I took the history of India, the literature of India, the politics of India and the language of India. In India, there are as many languages as there are states. So, I took Hindi, not to be confused with Hindu, which is the predominant and official religion of the country. One might ask why not Vietnamese? And the answer is simple: it was not offered at the U of I. In fact, of the 60 hours I needed to graduate, 59 of them were on Asia and 1 was a gym course. I needed four hours of gym to graduate, and I only had three hours. Gym wasn't my favorite subject, but a kind counselor suggested archery would be a good fit and she was right. Although, I did not replicate Gerry's childhood experience with Alice. No William Tell for me.

During the second semester of my junior year, I was offered the opportunity to apply for a National Defense Fellowship to study Hindi during the summer of 1968. The two colleges offering the fellowship were the University of Michigan and the University of California at Berkeley. I applied to both, and lo and behold, I was accepted at both. Coming from the Midwest, I immediately jumped at the chance to go to California, my reasoning being I had been all over Europe but had never been west of the Mississippi! Another more practical reason was that Berkeley was on the quarter system, which meant I could take a full course load of 15 hours and 12 of those hours would transfer back to the U of I, which was on the semester system. If that makes no sense, just take my word for it. That's how the system worked in 1968.

Now, the summer of 1968 was a very interesting time in the course of world history, and Berkeley, a hub for political protests, was the perfect place to observe the repercussions of these happenings. In May, a general unrest in France spearheaded by students, and eventually by blue-collar workers, closed the Sorbonne in Paris and factories in and around Paris. This resulted in clashes between the students, the workers, and the police, effectively shutting down the city for a month. Meanwhile, as the world was watching the Czechoslovakian people crawl out from under the oppression of Russian rule, the so-called Prague Spring, led by Dubcek, was coming to the attention of the Russian government, which invaded the country with military force, making the point of subjugation in the form of tanks rolling down the main street in Prague. And let's not forget the Democratic Convention in Chicago where tens of thousands of protesters gathered outside the convention hall, protesting the Vietnam War, while, inside the convention hall, the delegates were duking it out on that very same subject. The pro-war candidate won inside the convention hall, and the protesters clashed with the police outside the hall. The result was numerous protesters were arrested, seven of which were tried for conspiracy and inciting to riot. These seven were known as the Chicago Seven.

My introduction to Berkeley was protests in the streets for solidarity for the French students, which went on and off most of June. July was fairly quiet, but in August, we saw more protests for solidarity for the Czechoslovakian people, followed by solidarity for the Chicago protesters and the Chicago Seven. There were literally streets that you dared not walk down for fear of getting in the middle of a protest. In fact, I was walking around the neighborhood where I lived, memorizing Hindi vocabulary for my final, when I walked into a roadblock and a couple of policemen in riot gear. They demanded to know why I was there, and I answered that I was studying for a test and was not paying attention to where I was going. And now that I think about it, I was lost. They asked me for my address and when I told them, they pointed me in the right direction and told me to keep walking. I guess my kilt, knee socks, and Bass Weejun loafers didn't fit the picture of a person going to a riot!

In the house where I had an apartment, there lived a young couple with a young baby who was about nine months old. They were fashionably Marxist; I say fashionably because Ben's father was the American

Council to some African country and Susan, his wife, just didn't seem like the type. Anyway, they said they were going to the Black Panther Convention and asked if I would like to come. The Black Panthers were very active on campus, and I was intrigued by all the fuss, so I said sure. After all, I was a political science major. The convention was being held in a movie theater on Mission Street in San Francisco. We went early because they were holding an information 'fair' before the actual voting would take place. That interested me because we would get to meet some of the leaders of the Black Panther Party. I met Eldridge Cleaver, who was running for president and who had written a best seller book entitled *Soul on Ice*, and Dick Gregory, a comedian I had seen on the Jack Paar Show. I'm sure I met others, but the atmosphere was such that I felt unwelcome and out of place, so I just basically kept to myself. Finally, they opened the doors to the theater, and we all filed in and took seats. Someone announced that ballots and pencils would be passed out after the doors were closed. Ben and Susan had brought their baby, and I was holding her when suddenly, down both sides of the outside aisles of the theater, the Black Panthers filed in. They were an impressive sight with their black leather jackets and black berets. What did not impress me was the fact that every single one of them, both men and women, were carrying automatic weapons. I looked at Susan and asked, "This doesn't bother you?"

She replied, "No."

I said, "Well, it bothers me, so, if you don't mind, your baby and I are going to wait outside."

She said it was OK with her and I clutched the baby and walked out of the theater. Now, the theater was on Mission Street, which was a rough part of San Francisco, and just about the time I was wondering if I had jumped out of the frying pan into the fire, out came Ben and Susan. Without a word, we all walked to the car and left.

One funny thing that happened to me which I'm sure wasn't po- litically correct then and certainly isn't politically correct now was as a result of my inability to pronounce a certain 'd' in Hindi. The graduate assistant teaching the class, who was from Delhi, one of the northern states in India, was determined to get me to pronounce the word correctly. Consequently, he kept making me pronounce the word over and over. I have this theory that if you say your own name over and over enough times, you will mispronounce it, eventually. After about three times, the word I was trying to say was unintelligible and I admit some tears were shed. After class, the assistant, feeling sorry for me, walked me to my next class, and I attempted to explain why I could not pronounce that sound. I told him that maybe it was difficult for me because my father was Italian, and my mother was from the Deep South. My reasoning was that both Italian and the southern accent utilize broad open sounds, and the Hindi sound I was trying to pronounce was tight and guttural. The assistant, wide-eyed, looked at me and in all sincerity asked, "Is your mother a Negro?" Astonished, I just said I didn't feel he got my explanation!

About two weeks before the quarter was finished, my mother contacted me and told me that Gerry was in the United States and gave me his number so I could get a hold of him. I called him and he told me he was in Maine, working for his friend Mert, selling real estate, while he was negotiating for the management job in Vietnam. He told me it was a pretty good deal; they had given him a Cadillac convertible to his specifications, and he was staying in Mert's Maine cabin. The only thing he did not like was that there was this gorgeous oak tree in the middle of the plots of land he was selling, and he was told to use the tree as a selling point for the various properties. However, the tree was never on the property when the survey came back at closing. This fact did not sit well with Gerry, and he was beginning to wonder just who 'they' were.

While I was studying for my finals on the West Coast, two simultaneous events were happening on the East Coast. One: Gerry was notified by the New York office of Chrysler that his conditions were met, and he had the management position in Vietnam, so he needed to get to Vietnam as soon as possible. And two: my mother had invited Gerry for dinner as a surprise to me the evening I returned from California. Gerry packed up and called the real estate office to ask where he should turn in the car and was told that the car was his in lieu of future commissions owed him. He thanked them and immediately went to a used car lot to sell the car, only to be told that the car was stolen. Gerry now figured out who 'they' were! Rather than get involved in the whole mess of having a stolen vehicle, Gerry notified his contacts in Turkey (remember George?) and arranged for the car to be shipped to Turkey and disposed of. He then went to New York and reported to the CMS office to finalize the arrangements, book his flight, and do all the last-minute things one does when they are leaving. Ironically, as I was at the airport in LA getting ready to leave California for Chicago, Gerry was already on his way to Vietnam. When Gerry's plane had a layover in Beirut, Lebanon, he remembered that he had forgotten to tell my mother that he would not be coming for dinner. So, he called her and when he told her he was calling from Beirut, she thought he meant Beirut, Ohio, and told him he could still make dinner. The rest of the call consisted of a geography lesson as to where Lebanon was located!

I returned home with 15 credit hours from Berkley and the University of Illinois applied 12 towards my degree, leaving me 12 hours or one semester short of graduation. By the middle of January 1969, I was a graduate of the University of Illinois with a Bachelor of Arts in Political Science, and a Minor in Asian Studies.

Back In Vietnam

Letters from Gerry were few and far between. In fact, I don't think he ever wrote me any letters, at least, not any that I saved until right before I left for Vietnam. The first was right after Christmas. I was still on Christmas break and working at a gift shop that my cousin managed. My mother called me and told me I had just received a letter from Gerry. I said, "Great, I'll read it when I get home this evening." The next thing I knew, my father showed up in a snowstorm with the letter. "Read it," he said. "What does it say?"

Dear Judy,   *26 Dec 68 Saigon, V.N.*

I hope you enjoyed your Xmas, tried to call you but the lines were out between here and Hawaii. I had a big Xmas party, everybody was bombed, the next day the house looked like it went through a VC attack.

Now that you are finally finishing your school, I certainly hope that you will join me here in Vietnam. If you remember those were the plans that we had when we parted. I shall be here at least one more year. Of course, we will go on vacation for at least one month in June or July. Every once in a while, a person has to leave here just for the change in climate. I think you would enjoy it here; it certainly is different. This living is not bad, I have a very nice house, maid, car, plus there is plenty to do if you want to go out. I sometimes wonder if there is really a war here or if the war is back in the States. It is something a person must see for himself to really get any insight at all. Jobs are plentiful if you decided to work, all your major American companies and government agencies are here.

Please write ASAP what you have decided to do giving me details as to when you want to leave. I will then send you the ticket for the flight. The only thing you need for VN is a 30-day tourist visa which you must apply for in the US.

My feelings for you have not changed and I would certainly be glad to have you with me again.

Love, Gerry

P.S. Give my regards to your family.

I read the letter and told Dad it said to give his regards to the family and that he had invited me to come to Vietnam as soon as I graduated.

So, there it was, I knew we planned on me coming to Saigon after graduation, but now I had it in writing. Now I had some thinking to do. On January 10, 1969, Gerry wrote me another letter after I had expressed my doubts about going to Vietnam, and if I went, the timeframe of making the trip. My thoughts were that I needed to make enough money in the States before going, to hold me over for six months of travel in Asia in case I didn't want to stay in Vietnam. I had applied to grad school and was accepted at the University of Illinois in the Cultural Anthropology PHD Program, which would start in September 1969. I figured I needed at least $600 before I left.

Dear Judy,

Excuse the stationery as I have just disembarked from a plane from one of my upcountry trips. I realize that you may have some doubts about coming to Vietnam, although I can vividly remember a little girl that I once met on a ship going from Athens to India on $100 a month and she was very determined to do so. Of course, as you mentioned, people can change in 2 years. Judy, let me get to the point; as you well know, I am very bad at writing love letters, and I am also bad at expressing my feelings, but I always thought that when you finished your education, we would get together again. Whether or not I still love you or whether you love me, we certainly cannot tell, especially on paper, but I guess other people take chances and have a lot less to go by than we do.

Of course, I want you to understand that if your feelings are against it or you love somebody else or you feel that you have lost your 'wanderlust,' please don't do anything to please me. In other words, don't do me any favors. You must make up your own mind. You're grown up now, finished school, and have to make your own decisions. You probably think I am trying to be nasty but believe me, I am not. As far as I am concerned, I don't think I have changed. I always have these illusions of settling down somewhere, but it never happens. I still like to travel too much.

You should not worry about the expense of coming over because if you really want to come, I will gladly pay for it, including the round trip, which is only a formality and if you decide to stay, we can cash the ticket in. I won't have you sitting around the house as work is plentiful here with good money, and besides, you would be bored to death as I am on the road about 10 to 12 days a month. Please decide and let me know. I would love to see you, answer ASAP, so that I can cable the ticket to you. I will purchase it here at Pan Am and have your Pan Am office contact you.

This will probably be one of your first big decisions in life, so make it. Give my regards to your family.

Love, Gerry'

In order to make $600 as fast as possible, I got a job at the local stationery store, warning them that I had applied to Chrysler Corporation for a position overseas, so I could quit in three months without any hard feelings, inasmuch as I knew the owners and didn't want them mad at my family. I then got a job at Great Lakes Naval Training Center as a cocktail waitress in the evenings, which was my ole standby job. Between the two jobs, I had no trouble accumulating the $600 and then some that I needed before leaving for Vietnam. After telling Gerry I had decided to go to Vietnam, we found out that I actually needed a ticket in order to obtain a tourist visa. And much to my father's satisfaction, the ticket also had to exit Vietnam. Thus, I received my third and last letter from Gerry.

Dear Judy,   *5 Feb 69*

By the time this letter reaches you, you should have your ticket. I wired it to Pan Am USA c/o your address, the PTA # is 026900061816. The Pan Am travel agent here advised me to buy the ticket Chicago, Saigon, Bangkok, which enables you to leave Saigon; therefore, you are eligible for the 30-day tourist visa. For the extension, don't worry, as I have 30 people working for me and I am used to handling the extensions.

Smallpox shots are mandatory, also recommended is tetanus, ty-phoid-typhus, plague, and flu. (As an aside for 2021, this was called a vaccination record in the ole days! No such thing as an infringement of the traveler's rights!!) The average temp here is 85 to 90 year-round, so bring only light summer clothes. Your minis are accepted, after all, it is civilized and no worse than Turkey.

Judy, believe me, if I thought that there was any danger in you coming over here, I would be the last person in the world to tell you to come. This whole thing is sometimes a big farce and the newspaper buildup in the US doesn't help, but if they do not show violence, people would not be reading about the VN war. Please convey this to your parents and sisters and brothers, as I am sure that they are worried about you coming over here. Also, I might be loose-footed, but I am not crazy enough to live in a place where I am knowingly going to get killed.

Please cable me approx. 5 days before arrival, giving flight no. and day so that I can meet you. My cable address is CHRYNEWCAR Saigon, my address is 23 Gia Long office #13, Tel PTT 92744. My home address is Troung Minh Gian 264/I Tel Home PTT 24613.

I hope to see you soon, and don't get too excited and forget everything.

Love, Gerry

VIETNAM

When Gerry interviewed with Arnold Weber in Frankfurt, there was an instant bonding. Arnold knew he had found the one man who he could trust to run his Vietnam operation, and Gerry had found the second man in his life who would become his mentor.

The job started out simple enough. Gerry was given the Cholon PX in Saigon as a base of operation and 12 salesmen to escort to Saigon and place in various PX locations around Vietnam. As Gerry told it later, escorting 12 salesmen from Frankfurt to Saigon was a little like herding cats. First, the plane had a layover in Madras, India, now known as Chennai. Because India was a dry country, tourists who wanted an alcoholic drink had to fill out a paper declaring themselves alcoholics. Seems some of Gerry's salesmen actually thought that paper was an instruction manual and the plane was held up until a couple of them could be found and put back on the plane to continue the flight to Saigon.

Vietnam in 1967 was a war zone, and sadly, there were over 55,000 US personnel lost. But of all the car salesmen that went over between 1967 and 1973, only one man was lost. And, of all the cars and motorcycles that were sold under Gerry's management, only two deals were lost due to the death of the customer! So, Vietnam was a mixed dichotomy of ugly war and crazy partying a la the movie, *M*A*S*H*. Gerry's Vietnam experiences were 99% *M*A*S*H* stories.

One of Gerry's men, who was stationed on the DMZ, entertained the men in the officer's club by standing on his head on the bar and drinking pints of beer. This feat was amusing until the general walked in and ordered him to cease and desist. In complying with the order, he expelled the beer all over the man's medals. He apologized profusely and his apology, coupled with his suave British manners and British accent, plus the fact that he was an excellent salesman, kept him on the base. In fact, he went on to replace Gerry as manager of Panama years later when we finally left Chrysler and moved to the States.

He had another of his men, a retired British paratrooper, who decided to help the US military and march into Cambodia with them at the same time that President Nixon was on national TV assuring the US public that we were not in Cambodia. The British Embassy was not amused with this one.

One of Gerry's men stole an M151 Jeep and went out on the town drinking somewhere up country. He was sneaking onto the base early the next morning with his headlights off when he hit a column of Vietnamese army soldiers going out on patrol. He seriously injured three or four of the men. Gerry was called to handle the situation, i.e., get the guy out of the country. When Gerry confronted the guy, his excuse was he was only going three miles an hour. Gerry's reply was, "It must have been 'a steady three miles an hour!' "

Gerry had an Italian salesman on Binh Hua, an air force base just outside of Saigon. The base should have produced a large number of car sales but was far below projections.

One night, Gerry sat straight up in bed and exclaimed, "Silvio (the salesman's name) has a snake."

I asked him what he was talking about, and he said that, at the last sales meeting, Silvio had told him that he had a pet snake. The next day, Gerry drove to the base and sure enough, Silvio had this large, black snake coiled on his desk! Not exactly a way to attract customers!

Gerry had some warm/fuzzy stories, too. He hired a salesman who was discharged from the service and stayed in Vietnam. When Gerry asked him why he stayed to be a car salesman, he replied that his goal was to make $25,000 and go to graduate school at the University of Florida to get his PhD in History. He figured it would take a year. With no sales experience, Gerry didn't think he had much of a chance, but he was not going to be the one to take his dream away. Well, eight months later, the young man came into Gerry's office and quit, saying he had the money for graduate school and had been accepted at the University of Florida. By this time, Gerry acknowledged that he was a good salesman and tried to persuade him to stay, but the guy was adamant. Two-and-a-half years later, Gerry received a graduation announcement from this young man, saying he had received his PhD summa cum laude, with a note thanking Gerry for believing in him.

Sailing and waterskiing were two popular sports in Vietnam. The Mekong River ran from Saigon all the way to the South China Sea. There was a French boat builder in Vietnam, Andre Sangh, making power boats similar to old Chris-Crafts. The military was always good for outboards, and for the adventurous and anyone who had two water ski ropes tied together, there were always the PBRs (Patrol Boats, River). Gerry and a couple of his friends decided to go waterskiing one afternoon, not down the Mekong towards the South China Sea, but up the Mekong, towards Cambodia. They took a PBR for this adventure, mainly for the thrill of the wake and the machine guns attached, just in case.

Now, Gerry is Canadian, and the Vietnam war was not a war but a police action. *Don't you just love politicians?* Canada was part of the UN's peacekeeping mission, and as such, its embassy was in Hanoi. So, all the Canadians in South Vietnam were administered to by the British Consulate in Saigon. The morning after the waterski incident, Gerry got a call from the British vice-consul, who happened to be a friend of his. However, he invited Gerry to come to the consulate for 'a cup of tea.'

That particular invite had always meant trouble, so Gerry went, wondering what was wrong. When he got there, the vice-consul explained that he wanted to read him a report.

It said, "Big boat, then nothing for 50 meters, then man on board."

"Do you know what that means, Gerry?" the vice-consul asked.

Gerry replied, "It sounds like someone waterskiing behind a PBR; is that a problem?"

The vice-consul said, "Ordinarily, it wouldn't be; except, this was intercepted from the Khmer Rouge transmitting to somewhere in Phnom Penh. Apparently, the boat was in Cambodian waters. Next time someone decides to use a military boat to go waterskiing, could they please point the boat towards the South China Sea!"

We had friends living on a 40-foot Cheoy Lee sailboat, built in Hong Kong and moored at the Saigon Yacht Club. Every Sunday, if they were not our guests at Tien Yea, the yacht club's Sunday brunch island, we would sail down the Mekong River on their sailboat. One Sunday, we picked up Jeri, the wife. Her husband, Don, was on a flying mission. He was a pilot with Air America and sometimes flew unscheduled missions at the request of the US military. We had a great time on Tien Yea and continued to party on the Cheoy Lee when we returned to the yacht club, picking up a few more friends along the way.

We used Don and Jeri's dinghy to go from the clubhouse to the boat. The party was going strong when Don came back from his mission. We were all having fun. Don had worked all day. He was tired and just wanted to unwind. Instead, he had 10 or so overly happy people on his 40-foot boat. Gerry, always the gentleman, started gently clearing out the partiers. Now, this consisted of putting two unsteady people plus Gerry in the dinghy and rowing them to the yacht club's pier and then returning for another two. Everything was going fine until almost the end when he loaded up the second-to-last couple, who were each over 250 pounds, neither of them feeling any pain.

Gerry put one on each end of the dinghy, got in the middle, and rowed to the pier. When he arrived, the gentleman, who was in the stern of the dingy, got out, creating an imbalance. Gerry got out to help the lady off the dinghy, and the bow of the dinghy started sinking into the Mekong River with the lady, who, by this time, had completely passed out.

Gerry grabbed the boat and tried to lift the lady out onto the pier, but the angle and her weight was against him. Gerry started to go into the Mekong River face first, holding on to the lady. This was witnessed by the dinner crowd at the yacht club, who were laughing so hard that no one came to help Gerry. That was until Don used his bullhorn and started yelling that someone better help Gerry or that lady was going to drown!

Partying was a popular pastime in Saigon. Most started with cocktails, dinner, after-dinner drinks, and then drinks and conversation until curfew. I think having a curfew made it easier to keep having parties. You knew that everything would be over at 11:30 or so because you had to be off the streets by midnight. This curfew wasn't like a 'my folks will ground me if I'm late' type of curfew, it was more like a 'you will get shot' kind of curfew. Or the best-case scenario, you will get arrested.

So, we would go to a party, but throwing caution to the wind, Gerry always had to be the last to leave, which would make me a nervous wreck. One time, we went to a dinner party where, for some reason, dinner was never served. As I discovered halfway through, Gerry's drinks were all doubles. The conversation, consisting of questions about Gerry's car sales business, was a little strange too. Mostly because it appeared he wanted details about what was happening on the base. Fortunately, as it was told about Gerry, he never let the facts interfere with a good story, especially facts about military bases. Instead, in true Gerry fashion, he kept them entertained with funny stories based on common knowledge.

At about 11pm, I started negotiating to leave, but our hosts kept encouraging us to stay. Finally, at 11:50pm, I managed to drag Gerry out of the house, and we took off for home. About two miles from our apartment, Gerry started driving slower and slower until he finally came to a dead stop, turned to me, and said he could not drive any further. He told me that I would have to drive.

I had never driven in Saigon, and I was afraid. So, I talked him into continuing. On we went at about 15 miles an hour. By the time we arrived at the apartment, we had acquired a retinue of three jeeps, one of US MPs, one of a Vietnamese MPs, and one of the Vietnamese Civilian Police. I got out of the car and told Gerry he was on his own, and I went up to the apartment.

I don't know what he told them, but about 45 minutes later, Gerry came up and said, "They were all nice guys," and asked if I would mind if he invited them all up for a drink. I said, "Absolutely NOT!" It was now around 2am and enough was enough. I guess wiser minds prevailed because when Gerry went downstairs to tell them they couldn't come up, or maybe to invite them all up, they had all left!

One of our friends, Bob, a West Point graduate, and an engineer who had attained the rank of major before getting out of the military, had commissioned a trimaran sailboat before he left Thailand and moved to Vietnam for a civilian job. When the boat was finished, he invited Gerry and Stan, another friend who was an engineer, to sail the boat back to Vietnam with him. They were looking for one more person to crew, and I volunteered Lee, the sergeant major (SGM) I worked with as the fourth crewman. I volunteered Lee because all I heard was him begging me to put in a good word for him to get on the boat. What I did not know was that after 30 years in the military, Lee had never had a passport and had no idea how to get one. He had been around the world as a 'guest' of the US Military. And although he loved to fish, it was only from a rowboat. He had never sailed on the open sea. Well I got him a passport, a ticket to Bangkok, and instructed him on how to catch a taxi to Pattaya Beach to "catch" the sailboat known as the Rominey Road.

One thing I neglected to tell Lee was how to dress. Gerry said that he arrived in a suit, white shirt and tie, just as they were pushing the boat off the sand to launch it in the Gulf of Siam. They were having a hard time getting the boat to the water when someone noticed the boat was still tied to the palm tree!

Gerry said Lee hopped aboard and when the boat got underway, the usually talkative Lee did not say a word until they were once again on land. The trip was supposed to take three days. I was supposed to meet the boat in Vung Tau on Saturday and sail up the Mekong River with them to Saigon. However, the second night out they were hit by a horrific storm where all they could do was tie down the tiller and one of them stand watch while the other three went down below to get some sleep. It was on Gerry's watch that between lightning flashes he thought he saw black cliff ahead. He woke Bob, hoping it was his imagination, but Bob confirmed they were heading for some cliffs. They woke the others and worked to head the other way and re-tied the tiller.

The next morning, the storm passed. They saw land on the horizon. Hoping it was Vietnam, or one of the islands off the country, they sailed to it. They were met, not by Vietnamese but by Cambodians. Three young men got on the trimaran. One had an M-16 used by the GIs in Vietnam, one had an SSK, a Swedish weapon, and the other had an Uzzi from Israel. It was hard to tell from the weapons which side the men were on, whether friendlies or the enemy. Stan immediately jumped between the men and yelled for Lee to grab his camera and take a picture, gleefully shouting, "Come on guys, we've been captured!" Since the 'captors' were smiling and posing, pictures were taken all around.

The crew were then marched to the Cambodian Commodore's quarters with their passports. At this point Lee finally began talking, complimenting the women for their outfits and the beauty of the island. He also asked the young men if the waters had any fish.

The Commodore started questioning the guys whether they had any weapons on board, which they did not, and why they were in Cambodian waters. They explained about the storm and said they were on their way to Vietnam. The Commodore was dubious, but the American passports helped. Gerry's Canadian passport didn't. Seems even though he had been on that island for years the Commodore was aware that the Canadian Embassy was in Hanoi. Hanoi was in North Vietnam, not one of the 'good guys'! So, the crew of the Rominey Road were held for two full days while the Commodore translated Gerry's passport from the French to English to Cambodian.

After the first night, when gunfire could be heard in the distance, Bob, as captain, approached the Commodore and demanded that as 'prisoners of war' they be protected at night. The Commodore thought for a few minutes, drew his gun, and handed it to Bob and said something that the guys took to mean "you're on your own."

While awaiting the painstaking translation process, Lee lived out his fishing dream. He fished and the women cooked. "At least we ate well" was Gerry's comment. The next morning the Commodore told the men they were released to continue on their journey, but under no circumstances were they allowed to return to Thailand. This was fine with them, however for all the wind they had sailing to the island, they had absolutely no wind to leave. They started up the little motor which all true sailors disdain, which got them offshore and into international waters before it died. Never to be revived again. Slowly drifting towards Thailand, they began making plans as to what they were going to do when they arrived without visas or tickets to leave the country. Plus they needed to figure out where they were going to store the boat, and most importantly, how Lee was going to explain being designated AWOL after 30 years of exemplary service!

At one point, Gerry took out a military air traffic map to figure out where they were and discovered that they were probably drifting over a bomb disposal area. This is an area in the South China Sea where the B-52s drop their bombs when their missions are aborted, so they don't land with a full payload. Gerry asked if the bombs were defused before they were dropped. Bob and Stan just laughed and told Gerry not to worry, fused or defused, when dropped from 20,000 feet it wouldn't matter. If one landed on them, they'd be gone no matter what!

Meanwhile, on Saturday I caught a ride to Vung Tau with Joe, Gerry's office manager, got a room right on the beach in an old French hotel, and waited for the boat to arrive. I didn't really expect them to arrive on Saturday, but by Sunday afternoon I was getting nervous. On Monday, I called my boss in Saigon and told him the boat wasn't in and I'd see him Tuesday. I then taxied over to the base to catch a C-130 up to Saigon. First I went to the MAC Unit to see if there were any reports of a sailboat involved in any enemy action. I was relieved to find out there were not.

When I got back to Saigon, the MPs gave me a bit of trouble getting off the Tan Son Nhut AFB. They wanted to see my pass to get off the base. When I told them I did not have one, they wanted to see my pass to get on the base. I told them I did not have that either because I flew onto the base. They thought I was being sarcastic. Eventually I called my boss and he explained the circumstances and they let me go. Seems a girl in a mini skirt has more pull on a small base at a seaside resort than a large base in a city!

Meanwhile, back to the Rominey Road, the guys finally got back to Pattaya Beach early morning, six days after they had left. They walked into the customs office minus visas with their story of storm, capture, and becalming. The custom official, who was obviously not used to handling anything except the most ordinary of situations, told them that he would let them into the country to go to Bangkok with their story and petition to get visas. He cautioned that they had better hurry as the office closed at 5pm. He did tell them he would call and tell the office they were coming. The guys packed their belongings, helped Bob store the boat, and hired a taxi to take them back to Bangkok. They arrived with an hour to spare. Upon arriving, they discovered that the official in Pattaya did not call ahead. No one knew they were coming, let alone their situation. But the official they had to see was a sailor, with pictures of sailboats under the glass on his desk and models of sailboats on the shelves in his office. If anyone would understand being at the mercy of weather, it was him. He issued the necessary visas to enter Thailand and to leave, along with paperwork for the boat to leave for Vietnam later.

After checking into the hotel, Bob realized that he had left one important thing on the boat. A diamond engagement ring he had purchased so he could propose to his girlfriend. In all the commotion when they were 'captured' in Cambodia he had slipped the ring in the knife box. So, he went outside and hired a taxi driver to drive to Pattaya and rip the knife box off the wall of the gallery of the trimaran and bring it back to Bangkok. Just as the guys were taking bets on whether the taxi driver would show up with the knife box and the ring intact, he arrived, knife box, ring and all.

The next day the sailors arrived back in Saigon, sans the trimaran, but with a good story! Gerry arrived with a black mustache that didn't look very real with his blond hair, now bleached almost white from the sun. The consensus was that it made him look much older than his 31 years. Deciding he agreed with everyone, and much to my relief, he decided to shave it before we went out one night. Funny thing was although he looked different, no one realized he had shaved off the mustache!

LIVING IN S.E. ASIA

Saying goodbye to my family was bittersweet. On one hand, I was excited to start the next chapter of my life, and on the other, I was traveling to the other side of the world, exactly 12 hours and a day away. I had no idea when I was going to see them again. No card from Dad this time. No one we knew was born in Asia, but remember how God has a way of laughing at us humans and our plans. I now have a Korean brother-in-law and a Philippina niece! My ticket was for March fourth, arriving in Saigon on the fifth. Although it was just a coincidence, I arrived in Saigon exactly two years to the day I met Gerry in Turkey!

The first custom I was introduced to in Vietnam was a type of tea ceremony. It was the first day I arrived and after a long nap, trying to beat jet lag which told me it was nighttime when in reality it was mid-morning, Gerry took me to a restaurant to meet a good friend of his, Chuck. After meeting Chuck, he kept telling me I would really like his wife, Joanne. Well, after a glass of wine, jet lag started creeping into my brain and Gerry and Chuck were deeply engrossed in a conversation about stocks, when a young lady sat down at the table. Both Gerry and Chuck greeted her effusively and introduced her to me, then went on with their conversation. The lady, whose name was Anne, was half French and half Vietnamese. We started talking about what I was doing in Saigon and what she was doing in Saigon—basically things two people who have just met each other talk about while getting to know each other.

While we were talking, the waiter came over to take our drink orders. I ordered another wine. Anne ordered tea. The guys ordered beer. As the conversation went on, Anne asked me several times if I would mind if she had another tea, and of course, I kept saying she should go ahead. So, she kept calling the waiter over to bring her more tea. The evening wore on and Anne left. I told Gerry I had to leave before I fell over from lack of sleep. He looked at his watch and said we should go anyway because it was almost curfew and he wouldn't want me to be shot on my first night in Saigon. That woke me up! They called for the bill. When they got it, they called the owner over and demanded to know why the bill had 20 teas on it. Seemed that Anne was the owner's daughter, not Chuck's wife as I'd thought. Every time she asked me if I minded if she had a tea, I was buying her a tea, which was one of the ways in which the tea girls made money. A 3-ounce glass of tea cost $1.00 (same as a beer) and the house split the cost with the girl. The owner told Gerry and Chuck that I bought the teas. They laughed and split the bill, and from that moment forward, I was known as the girl who bought teas for the tea girls!

As if that wasn't excitement enough for my first night in Saigon, at about 2 in the morning, I was awakened by some loud, horrific booms which seemed to surround Gerry's whole villa. Gerry told me they were the sound of the B-52s dropping bombs nearby. He told me not to worry; they were the good guys. He put his arms around me, and said even so, if we were going to die, at least we would die together.

I looked at him and said, "Speak for yourself. I'm 22 and I'm not in the mood to die. I'm going to Hong Kong tomorrow." I didn't go, but the first time I actually breathed a sigh of relief was in June when we did go to Hong Kong!

Within a week of arriving in Saigon, I started job hunting. Unfortunately, my job skills were minimal. With a BA from the University of

Illinois, there was very little I could do, so I ended up working at the PX behind the make-up counter, making $1.60 an hour plus overtime. This was an interesting job in itself. The week I started, the PX received a very large shipment of make-up. This fact wouldn't be unusual if I was working for Mary Kay, or Ulta Beauty, or even the make-up section of a drug store, but I was working for the make-up section of the PX in Vietnam, a country that was at war, and a military that had sent home all civilian dependents. Theoretically, I literally had no customers to sell to! I was told that each item in the shipment was rationed one per customer and every customer that purchased make-up had to be logged in on a sheet of paper by rank, name, and date purchased.

As soon as the doors of the PX opened, a line started forming at my counter, which eventually wound around the PX and out the door. I swear I got to meet every officer in the Royal Thai Army from captain down, all carrying the guns they took into battle.

One soldier, resenting the rationing process, said to me, "Why you do this? We all look alike to you!" I had no answer for that so I just smiled.

Working behind the make-up counter in Saigon was not my dream job, so I found out about a shorthand course AAFES (Army Airforce Exchange Service) was offering to any interested employee. I immediately signed up for the course, figuring if I could learn shorthand, I could apply for a secretarial position. I figured if I could master Hindi, Italian, and French, I could master shorthand. Well, just as I am not fluent in any of the mentioned languages, I am also not fluent in shorthand. But the advantage of shorthand was combining it with my years of note taking; I managed to fake my way into a secretarial position.

So, while Gerry was traveling from base to base, putting out fires, and keeping what eventually became his team of 42 salesmen in line, I went from the make-up counter to secretary of first a section chief then to secretary to the Major of Safety & Security. I received a secret clearance in this role. Eventually, mainly because I was the 'last secretary standing' with a secret clearance, I became secretary to the Commander of the Vietnam Regional Exchange. This position, with my poor shorthand skills, could have intimidated most individuals but along the way, I had discovered an important lesson. As long as you get the gist of what the speaker wanted to say, and all the words are spelled correctly, and grammatically correct, he will sign off on the letter or round table notes! To quote Gerry, "The world is run by the guy in the basement with the green visor." I was that guy!

I had been in Vietnam for three months when, true to his word, Gerry took me on a trip to visit more of Southeast Asia. Our first stop was Hong Kong, where, as I said earlier, I was able to finally breathe. We met his mother in Hong Kong and the three of us did the tourist thing. Even though Gerry had been living in Asia for two plus years, he had never stopped to smell the roses, so he was just as interested as his mother and me to see the sights. Hong Kong was a shopping mecca in those days (1969), so of course, we indulged. The most well-known department store was called Crawford's, which was equivalent to Harrods in London and Macy's in New York. We purchased a fondue set, which we sent to our military address in Vietnam. I do not know the logistics of the mailing process, but I remember it took six months to get there. We still have that fondue pot but as it is heated by sterno, it was replaced by one that is heated by electricity a long time ago, although the forks are still in use! And today the pot sits on one of our shelves as a curiosity of a former life!

Our tourist excursion consisted of taking the Peak Tram up the Peak to view Hong Kong's harbor, the Central District, and the hills of Kowloon, at 1,305 feet above sea level. It is touted as one of the dozen or so great sights of the world. We then walked down the hill, viewing all the islands in the South China Sea towards Macao and hailed a taxi to visit the old Chinese fishing village of Aberdeen, where the people live on their fishing boats. One night, we took an evening tour of the harbor on a sunset cruise, visiting the harbor, Aberdeen, and several islands, complete with romantic music and copious drinks.

Our visit to Hong Kong was the first of many. It was centrally located and had good shopping opportunities; in fact, I had my bridal dress made there, and eventually we even had friends, who owned a renovated authentic Chinese junk, living there.

After Hong Kong, we stopped in Taiwan, where Gerry visited an acquaintance who was selling fabric. He showed us some fabric that he thought Gerry should buy and have a suit made. He said the tailors in Taiwan did fabulous jobs and to prove it he pointed to the suit he was wearing. We looked, we passed, not on the tailoring job, but the material!

While we were at the PX, Gerry introduced me to another man he'd bumped into, who worked in car sales in Vietnam for a rival company. I paid no attention to his name, as he did the same to me, but we politely shook hands.

After Hong Kong, Taiwan was not that exciting from a tourist point of view. We spent one-and-a-half days there, and frankly, the American PX was the most interesting thing we visited.

Our next stop was Japan, which we all were looking forward to visiting. We booked a tour to see the city because Tokyo was so big that if you called a taxi, the taxi would only take you as far as he knew, then you would have to call another taxi to take you further. Gerry had heard about this, but he thought it was an old wives' tale. He'd promised someone in Vietnam that he would buy a part for their Honda; three taxis later, he finally found a Honda shop that sold parts! You'd think buying a part for a Honda in Japan would have been an easy thing!

The tour took us to the Tokyo Imperial Palace Plaza, the National Diet Building, several shrines, the Komazawa Olympic Park built for the 1964 Olympics, several beautiful gardens, the University of Tokyo, the business district, and finally, and most importantly, the Ginza and Takashimaya (the Macy's of Japan!). When we got to the end of the tour, the tour guide called off our names, to ensure we all arrived back (we used tickets to get on the tour). When he got to our names, he called off Mr. and Mrs. Harles (Gerry and his mother!), then he looked at my name—Vignocchi, my maiden name—and after a long pause, called out, "And one other lady." Unfortunately, for the rest of the stay in Japan, I became 'one other lady!' As we got off the bus and walked to our hotel, Mrs. Harles almost tripped over something on the sidewalk. She reached down, picked it up, and gave it to Gerry. It turned out to be the yen equivalent of $360. When we got back to the hotel, we told the concierge that we had found some money, who told us that until another guest reported missing the money, we should just keep it.

Our last stop on our tour of Asia was the Philippines, where Gerry had some business with his boss, Arnold Weber. His mother was returning to Germany $360 richer! I was left to my own resources, so I immediately decided to go shopping. I had been told that the best deals on shoes in Asia could be found on Carriedo Boulevard. So, I took a taxi to the area and went shopping. After purchasing two pairs of very glamorous sandals, I started to look for a taxi when I was surrounded by a group of young men.

I attempted to ignore them until one of them put his hand under my skirt. I immediately swung around, hit him with my shoe boxes, and ran like hell into the middle of the street, where there was a policeman directing traffic. I asked him to help me get back to my hotel. He explained that it was lunchtime for most of the taxis, but he could put me on a jeepney if I was willing to pay all the fares that the driver would lose taking me alone. While I was agreeing to this, the group of young men approached the policeman with a complaint against me. Apparently, when I swung the shoe boxes, I hit the miscreant in the eye, making his eye really swell up, and they wanted me to pay them. I ignored the group, hopped on the jeepney, and told the driver to take me to the Manila Hilton.

Well, the ride was not the solo experience that I anticipated when I got in. First, every time the driver stopped at a stoplight, people got on.

Added to that, the miscreants hailed their own jeepney and followed me. I finally got to the hotel—after making friends with all my fellow passengers. I hopped out, gave the driver the amount of money we had agreed upon, and as I walked into the hotel, I asked the concierge to take care of the 'mob.' I then found Gerry and Arnold and told them I had had a little trouble in town. By the time I finished, the concierge had found them and asked Gerry to please go out and take care of the 'mob.' It probably cost Gerry more than I spent on the sandals, but I never asked. Every time I wore the sandals, though, I thought of Manila and the deals you could get on Carriedo Boulevard!

After a few days in Manilla, it was time to return to Saigon and the war. I remember the whole airport was abuzz with the news that Neil Armstrong had walked on the Moon, and Miss Philippines had been crowned Miss Universe. I don't know who the Filipinos were most proud of, the United States' accomplishment or Miss Philippines' victory! The day is engrained in my mind—July 20, 1969.

Saigon wasn't all work and war and no play. After I arrived, Gerry decided a nice diversion would be to join the Saigon Yacht Club (thus the sailing stories earlier). Well, we knew where the yacht club was located, at the end of Tu Do Street on the river, but we weren't sure where the 'island' location of the club was. (Called such because everyone in their right mind either motored or sailed to the spot.) Gerry heard that there was a way to drive to the location, and one Sunday, we decided to find out how.

We found the road, it being the only one that went east off the main highway, but we had a hard time finding the entrance to the old Club Nautique. The main reason we were having so much trouble, world travelers that we were, was the fact that the road had been mined several times and it wound around the damages. We got to a place which Gerry was sure led to the entrance, and after driving about 10 car lengths into the area, we immediately got the car stuck. To make matters worse, the only thing that came over to help us was something that we hadn't seen when we drove in: a very large water buffalo.

Now, water buffalo are like pets to the family of the farmer who owns them, but feeling threatened by some foreigners in a beige Mazda in his field, he lost his friendliness! Fortunately, after a few forward and backwards motions, Gerry got us unstuck, and we backed out of the water buffalo's field and got back on the road. We never did find the entrance that Sunday, but Gerry decided to get a boat and approach the club from the water.

In December 1970, Gerry had an incident with one of his salesmen that directly affected my future. The salesman, who will remain anonymous, took a home leave, and returned to England to visit his folks. He stopped along the way at every PX between Saigon and London, and a few in England as well, and purchased all sorts of hi-fi and camera equipment, along with a diamond engagement ring. He paid for everything with checks on a closed account and proceeded to return to Saigon with all his purchases. Fortunately for Gerry, this incident caught up with him while he was still in Saigon awaiting a military hitch to go up country to his post. Arnold was in Saigon and he and Gerry decided to pay a visit early one morning to this salesman and relieve him of as much of his ill-gotten gains as was possible to cover his bad checks. The mission was successful, and Gerry and Arnold were able to sell the goods, all except the diamond engagement ring, which Gerry said he wanted to buy to give to me as proof that we were engaged. Remember, this was over 50 years ago, and engagement rings were necessary things to 'seal the deal' as far as marriage went. They decided on $125 as a fair price, but Arnold said it would be better if I purchased the ring, since Chrysler Military, who had to make up the shortfall between what the goods were sold for and what they cost, might think there was hanky-panky if Gerry bought the ring. The New York office wouldn't know who Judy Vignocchi was. So, that's how I purchased my own engagement ring.

To carry this story to its conclusion, in 1971, after we set the date for our wedding, Gerry ordered the wedding band to go with the engagement ring from the PX. Unfortunately, by the time the ring was ready for pickup, third country nationals or non-USA citizens had lost their PX privileges, and I had to pick up and pay for the wedding band as well, which cost me $35. A total of $160, not a bad investment for almost 50 years of marriage!

In the five years we lived in Vietnam, we were able to go skiing twice at Shiga Kogen in the Japanese Alps, and once to Thredbo in the Snowy Mountains in Australia. My first skiing experience was in Japan, and except for the first day, when Gerry gave me some rudimentary pointers, I spent the rest of the time skiing alone on the trails and feeling sorry for myself. But I must admit, the après ski was worth it, especially after I twisted my ankle and everyone felt sorry for me! The place we skied in Japan was famous for its hot springs and the basement of the hotel had numerous private rooms to enjoy them. The first night, Gerry asked me if I wanted to experience them the way the Japanese did, and I foolishly said yes, so, upon getting out of the spring, which was almost too hot, he threw a bucket of cold water on me. Well, after my heart resumed beating, I informed him that if he ever did that again, it was all over between us!

Fate has a way of getting even, however. On our second trip to Japan, which I enjoyed far more, having taken ski lessons in Australia, Gerry broke his hand leaning on his ski pole waiting for me to catch up. This did not deter Gerry from skiing since the resident doctor at the hotel was a skier himself. Gerry merely had him form the cast in such a way that he could grip a ski pole. Of course, when we got back to Saigon, one of our friends, who was an orthopedic surgeon, under the guise of looking at his hand to see what the Japanese doctor had done, rebroke his hand and applied a proper cast.

But that's not the end of the story. The base of the cast was an aluminum rod that ran along Gerry's arm, around which gauze was wrapped and then casting material applied. Because he could not play golf with his hand in a cast, he took up tennis. Gerry managed to pull the rod out of the cast long enough to form it into a hook which could hold two tennis balls. The end of this story is a moral of cause and effect. Eventually, playing tennis in the unbalanced state of having a cast on one arm gave Gerry bursitis in his hip, necessitating a shot of cortisone!

For my first Christmas in Vietnam, I ordered a Christmas tree from the Sears and Roebuck catalog, along with a garland and ornaments. We assembled the tree and decorated it on Christmas Eve as was the custom in my family. On Christmas day when our maid, Angelique, came to work (she insisted, not our requirement) she admired the tree, and Gerry explained how the tree could be taken apart and put back in the box to be used next year. With that said, we told Angelique to go home and enjoy the holiday and we went to our friends the Grewers to celebrate. The Grewers lived in a large villa, consisting of three stories. Chuck, his wife, Joanne, and three children lived on one floor, and Terry, his brother, lived with his wife, Sandy, on the top floor. They had a dog named Spike who lived wherever he wanted.

While we were having cocktails, Spike helped himself to the Christmas dinner, leaving us with some sides that were not to his taste and a large bowl of Chinese noodle soup that Terry's wife made.

To make matters worse, Spike, curled up nose to tail, farted, and looked up at us as if we did it and disgustedly walked off!

Upon arriving home, we found our Christmas tree neatly taken apart and put back in the box it came in. So much for communication between Gerry and Angelique. That was our first and last Christmas in Saigon, as we celebrated the holiday out of the country for the next three years. We ended up selling the tree as almost new when we left the country in 1973!

CAMBODIA

In May 1971, as the US president went on TV and declared to the American people that there were no US troops in Cambodia, we decided to visit Phnom Penh, Cambodia, over Memorial Day weekend. At this time, the Cambodian army was involved in fighting the Khmer Rouge, which closed the supply route from the Gulf of Siam into the city. But because of the US involvement, the city itself was relatively safe. What was not safe, as we discovered 30 days later, were the oysters we consumed in abundance at La Taverne.

At any rate, we did have a great time visiting the city with its many wonders as well as the surrounding area. Back in those days, one's camera equipment, if they were well prepared, and we were, consisted of a camera, a wide angle and telephoto lens, as well as various filters, carried around in a large bag. To the Cambodians, we represented the press, and everyone wanted to show us their treasures as well as have us take their picture.

We visited an imposing temple on the outskirts of Phnom Penh which had a grand staircase leading to the entrance, with 'handrails' designed like cobras. As we got closer to the staircase, I saw an actual cobra on the bottom step with his hood unfurled just like the stone cobras. I told Gerry to quickly take a picture. He aimed, focused, and froze. We stayed there long enough for the real cobra to lose interest and slink away, and I discovered Gerry had a weakness; he was not impressed with snakes! He was my Indiana Gerry!

Thirty days later, I started feeling really tired and food started tasting like cotton batten. My boss said I must have picked up something 'on the economy' and sent me to a field unit to be checked out. The doctor examined me and asked if it hurt when she massaged my stomach. I told her it did, and she asked to see my eyes (I was wearing sunglasses). I told her they were probably red because I had been scratching them all morning. She told me they were not red, but bright yellow. I had hepatitis. She asked me if I had eaten any seafood recently. She then told me to report to the 3rd Field Hospital, while she arranged a room for me (the hospital was dormitory style for the wounded men). I asked her what would happen if I did not report to the hospital, and she said she would have the MPs pick me up. Well, at that time, I worked with a whole office of MPs, so I doubted that would happen. However, when I got back to the villa where we had our office, the major I worked for had already been notified that I was to report to the hospital.

I told Gerry about my diagnosis (his office was in the building next door), and he drove me home to pick up some necessities. He also reminded me that we knew a lot of the doctors and nurses at the hospital so not to worry about having to stay. We got to the hospital and looked up our friend, Stuart, who was a major and a cardiovascular surgeon. He explained why I had to stay. That was a week to remember. I got even sicker before I started feeling better and was so weak, I could scarcely walk to the washroom. They tested Gerry and found out he had walking hepatitis. All he had to do was take it easy.

There was a silver lining to the experience. I lost 21 pounds, thus looking thin and trim for our wedding that took place two months later. Since I was in the hospital over the Fourth of July, I got a tiny American flag on a stand to take home. That flag, atop a jar of peanut butter, witnessed many arguments between Gerry and our French friend, Patrick, over everything and anything about the American versus the French handling of the Vietnam War!

AUSTRALIA

Our only trip to Australia was essentially for business, but we took advantage of traveling 'Down Under' to also get in some skiing, so Gerry took his skis and boots. The skis caused quite a commotion leaving Saigon, since the only skis the baggage handlers had ever seen were waterskis. It was funny to see how one of the handlers was demonstrating how he thought the skis were used to waterski.

We flew from Saigon to Singapore, and then to Djakarta, where we were changing planes for the long flight to Sydney, Australia. Our flight landed in Djakarta at 11pm, and we were supposed to catch our flight at 12am. At approximately 11pm, the airport started closing down, shutting off lights and locking doors. We went to the Pan Am counter and asked about our flight, and the attendant told us there was not another flight expected that night. Gerry insisted the attendant call the Pan Am manager in Djakarta. After a bit of indignant discussion, the attendant got the manager on the line. Gerry told him that there had to be a flight as we had confirmed tickets. The manager told him that the flight schedule had changed, effective 1 July and the 12am flight had been eliminated. Just to be sure, he told us to go outside and see if there were any runway lights on. Since there were no runway lights lit, he said the plane was not coming. The mistake had been made by Saigon Pan Am as there had been a 12am flight on 30 June, but that was before we started our trip!

The bad news was that the next flight leaving Djakarta for Sydney was on Wednesday, which was three days from then; the good news was we would be able to take a tour of Djakarta! You have to understand, in those days, there was only one flight to choose from. We could not go to other airlines and book our trip. We took a taxi to the Hotel Indonesia and the next day, Gerry called the Pan Am office in Saigon and asked the manager, who was a friend, what he was going to do about our dilemma. Well, we did get our hotel and food paid for, but that didn't get us to Sydney any sooner and thus didn't solve our problem. The business part of the trip was for the purpose of recruiting more salesmen for Vietnam. Gerry was supposed to go early to place an ad for interviews. So, he had to call his boss, Arnold, and tell him we were going to be late. Arnold was in Thailand at the time, and the Thais and the Indonesians were fighting over fishing rights in the Gulf of Siam. Consequently, it was impossible to call Bangkok from Djakarta on a local line, so he had to call on a military line. This was easier said than done. He had to use a local line to call the military line in Hawaii. There, he could have the military call the military line in Thailand, which would in turn call the Thai PTT line. As complicated as this was, the snafu came when the Hawaii operator did not know where Indonesia was. As Gerry was explaining the geography of SE Asia, he became more and more frustrated. I am very happy to say, he did manage to hold his temper, and after one-and-a-half hours, he did make the call.

On Wednesday, we finally did catch our flight to Sydney. It was an overnight flight, so we had a luxurious dinner, a movie, and tried to get some sleep. About an hour before we landed, the stewardess started serving breakfast. Just as she was finished, the navigator came into the cabin and pressed a button in the ceiling and an instrument panel came down. With what appeared to be a map in his hand, he started fiddling with the buttons on the panel. After about two minutes, he turned the map around as if it had been upside down and did some more fiddling, then closed the panel and went back to the cabin. Needless to say, no one on the plane enjoyed their breakfast! But we did land with no major complications.

As Arnold had arrived before us, he had placed the ad and was ready to begin the interviews. While the men interviewed, I shopped for a ski outfit. Since our first trip to Japan skiing, I had worn my old parka and ski pants that I had worn in 1966 on my first trip to Europe.

Well, the recruiting did not go as expected as the only candidate that Gerry and Arnold felt was a possibility told them he had to 'check with his mum' first, and his 'mum' said no!

At least we got to go skiing in Thredbo in the Snowy Mountains. And I did find a great ski outfit.

After saying goodbye to Arnold, we started off on our ski trip, stopping first in Canberra to take a few pictures of the capital. We arrived at our hotel, and after checking in, we were told there was no porter, so we had to carry our own bags to the room. The man at the desk apologized and told us they did have a night porter, prompting Gerry to reply that people who check in at night only need a toothbrush!

Skiing at Thredbo was not the same as skiing in Shiga Kogan. First of all, there did not seem to be central heating at the hotel. Waking up that first morning, the water in the toilet was frozen—a new experience. Secondly, and most important to me, there was no warm fuzzy après ski. The bartender had never heard of hot buttered rum. When questioned, he offered a cognac, which by the way was cold! Back in those days (early '70s) the beer of the day was Dinner Ale, which the locals called 'Dirty Annie,' with good reason.

Going down to dinner that first evening, Gerry requested a table by a window, from where you could enjoy the mountains and the sunset, but was told that table was reserved for the owner of the hotel. Seemed like a reasonable explanation, except that for the whole five days we were there, the owner never appeared. But what took the prize in hospitality was that we were told that breakfast was from 8 to 10am. When we came down for breakfast at 9:50am, we were told that the kitchen was closed. Gerry nicely asked if we could at least have some toast and a couple of eggs but the waiter told us that the cook had left. When Gerry asked where he went, since the resort was miles from any other town, the answer was "he is just out." And so it went. We remarked that the Australians could learn a lot from the Japanese. However, the best oysters I have still ever eaten was atop the Wentworth Hotel in Sydney, and I didn't get sick!

WE SAY I DO

A little over halfway through our tenure in Vietnam, we went back to the States to get married. This joyous occasion was not without its incidents! The first of which was our arrival at US Customs in Hawaii. I was carrying my wedding dress in a large white box, which immediately attracted the attention of the custom official. He asked what it was and where I got it (we never opened the box). I told him it was my wedding dress, and it was made in Hong Kong. He told me I would have to pay customs on it. I protested, saying I had lived abroad for three years and basically everything except my underwear had been made in Asia. He started to open our suitcase and Gerry butted in and showed him his passport and said as a Canadian, he did not have to pay customs on his clothes when he visited the States. The custom official asked which was his suitcase, and Gerry told him both were his; we had packed together. The official changed the subject and told us the suitcases were OK, but if we did not want to pay customs on the dress, he could seal the box and ship it to the Canadian border, and we could pick it up when we left the States. After 18 hours on an airplane, I started to cry and Gerry exclaimed, in a loud voice, "Is it against the law for a Canadian to wear a wedding dress through customs?" He started taking off his sports coat, at which time everyone behind us moved to another line, and the custom official tried to mollify Gerry. When Gerry kept going by threatening to take off his trousers, the customs official backed down and told us to proceed out of the area. Incident handled!

The next incident that is still talked about today was the golf game between Gerry, my father, and two of Dad's golfing buddies. Remember, this was before we joined the golf club in Saigon and Gerry took golf lessons. Because this was the first time Gerry had ever played golf, he tended to hold up the game with the more experienced, to say the least, golfers. To speed up the game, every time Gerry got close to the hole, my father told him to pick up his ball, it was a 'gimmie.' So, not understanding the game, Gerry would pick up his ball and enter the number he was laying as his score. At the end of the game, as Gerry added up his score, he told my father that if he did not tell my family that he won, he would not marry me. Now, I have never known my father to ever lie. In fact, the only time he ever punished us was when he caught us lying. So, upon coming home, when Dad was asked who won, all he would say was "I didn't!"

Another noteworthy incident was at the church. We are Catholic, and back in those days, the church was very particular about both the bride and groom being baptized. Gerry had been baptized, but his mother either couldn't find the certificate, or never had one. The priest told my mother that was no problem if Gerry's mother would come with us to the pre wedding interview and state that Gerry had been baptized.

When we got to the interview, it was discovered that the priest's parents were also from Sudetenland, and he spoke German. After he asked me all the required questions, as a courtesy to Gerry's mother, he began to question Gerry in German. The first question was "are you entering this marriage of your free will?" Now, before I give you Gerry's answer, I have to explain, my parents were bastions of the parish. My mother was instrumental in running the annual rummage sale, and my father was the cantor of 10:30 Mass. My father was also a prominent member of the Knights of Columbus, an Italian Catholic men's club.

So, Gerry answered in German, "Well, Father, you know about Judy's father, right?"

The unsuspecting priest answered, "Of course."

Gerry then went on to explain that my father told him, if he didn't marry his daughter, he would put cement shoes on his mother and throw her into Lake Michigan. There was dead silence in the room. Mrs. Harles was sheet white and quivering in anger. My parents, although not understanding the words, sensed the tension in the room. Until the priest thought, then said in English, "Good one! Now let's be serious!" The laughter that followed cemented the story, to be retold often over the years.

For our honeymoon, we planned on driving from Lake Forest to Fairbanks, Alaska. Gerry's driving was renowned for its speed. He had flown to Detroit with my brother, Michael, to pick up a Chrysler he had special ordered prior to leaving Saigon. On our way, we planned on making a detour to Maine to visit one of his best friends, Mert.

Accompanying us on this trip was Gerry's mother, Mitzi. She flew into Chicago a week before we arrived from Vietnam and totally charmed my whole family. My aunt, Tina, even had her over for lunch and served Reuben sandwiches under the impression that because they had sauerkraut, they must be German. Maybe she was right for all I know! At any rate, Mitzi loved the lunch. We included Mitzi on our trip because she hadn't been back to Tomslake since she left in 1958. We thought she should return one time to see old friends and visit remembered places. It was an easy decision because one, Gerry and I had seen many places all over the world together, so it was not an issue to share this trip with Mitzi; and two, we had traveled with her before and enjoyed her company.

When Gerry called Mert to ask him how long he thought it would take us to get to Maine, Mert replied, "With Gerry's love of speed, it will take less time than the average person." But he cautioned Gerry to be careful, because he couldn't talk or bribe his way out of a ticket in the States. Gerry replied that if he was caught, he would show them his Canadian passport, speak German, and give them his Vietnamese driver's license! What could they do? Mert replied, "Throw your ass in jail."

Well, we arrived at Mert's house without any tickets. However, as we left Maine to continue our trip to Alaska, on driving through the province of Ontario, which was a three-day trip (stopping nights to have a good dinner and a good night's sleep), Gerry's foot got heavier and heavier until we passed a Royal Canadian Policeman. When we noticed he was following us with his lights on, Gerry attempted to slow down by pulling the hood release. He figured it would act as an air foil to slow us down—1971 was the first year the hood release allowed the hood to come completely up.

When we stopped, the hood came down. Gerry got out of the car, ran to the front, and tried to close it, but it was damaged and he was unable to completely close it. The policemen told us that he clocked us at 120 mph, but he wasn't in a position to give us a ticket, so he told us to report to the police station in Thunder Bay. He wrote out the information on a sheet of paper which he told us to give to the police there. Well, Thunder Bay was a good 100 miles from where we were. But since it was on the way, we drove there and discovered there was not any conspicuous police force presence. Instead, we found a park nearby and had a picnic lunch and drove on.

However, the 'fickle finger of fate' got us in British Columbia, where we were stopped once again for speeding and escorted to the police station. It was on a Friday, and Gerry had a choice. He could stay in jail until Monday when the judge was in court or pay a fine of $800 cash. Fortunately for us, traveling in Asia, where at that time credit cards were not widely used and checks were suspect everywhere except at American PXs, we were used to carrying cash. So, we had the money for the fine. We paid the fine and went on our way.

Our first stop for Mitzi was in Edmonton, Alberta, where we visited Dr. and Mrs. Glas. These were good friends of Mitzi's and Gerry's father.

Dr. Glas was the doctor who delivered Gerry. Unfortunately, Dr. Glas was in the hospital, so our visit was brief, consisting of an afternoon of cake and sweet wine! The ladies started reminiscing about coming to Canada, first by boat and then train to British Columbia. They remembered that at every stop of the train, Canadians met them with smiles and sandwiches. Although history proved that they were being sent to a desolate part of the country and expected to farm, an undertaking that was foreign to their way of life, all they remembered was the fact that 'the buns weren't crispy' on those sandwiches of long ago!

We visited Tomslake (also referred to as Dawson Creek) and saw Gerry's old home, and the barn built by his father and grandfather. We also visited some of his old friends. One asked if Gerry had been in jail, since he had been away for so long! We went to the home of a good friend of Mitzi's who showed us their latest acquisition—a flushing toilet! After leaving, we asked Mitzi if she was happy she came. Her response was that she was happier she had left.

Our next stop was in Whitehorse, which is the capital of the Yukon territory and the seat of the provincial government. As we entered the town, we saw a billboard welcoming visitors, signed by the governor, Keith Fisher-Fleming. Gerry got excited and said that he thought the governor was his old boss from the gas station. His original dream was to be the Governor of Hong Kong. We knew he had gone to law school and became a lawyer at the age of 72, but we had lost contact with him after that. Gerry said he was going to go to the administrative building the next day and find out. The following day, Gerry got ready to go. I told him I did not want to accompany him and be embarrassed, as I was sure he was wrong. So, Gerry went, and lo and behold, he found out the governor was his old boss, and he was able to get an appointment with him. They spent an hour catching up. So, Keith, while not being appointed to Hong Kong, did make it to the Yukon territory. It's really true, shoot for the moon, and even if you get a star, you're doing okay!

We left Whitehorse and took off for Alaska. Our plan was to visit Anchorage, and then go to Fairbanks, say goodbye to Mitzi, sell our car, and fly back to Vietnam. Back in 1971, the contrast between the two cities was like night and day. Anchorage was a beautiful city, which we enjoyed after mentally roughing it on the road between Whitehorse and Anchorage. With little to see except beautiful scenery and rough, rural, hut-like houses. But Fairbanks was like going back 70 years to the rough and tumble western town reminiscent of old cowboy movies. We had no trouble arranging for Mitzi's travel back to Germany. As for selling the car, well, things were done differently in Fairbanks.

Communication was difficult, and the inhabitants were spread so far apart that the most effective way of advertising was to put it on the radio. So, Gerry put the car on the radio, and I sat in the hotel's café listening for replies, while Gerry picked the most prominent neighborhood he could find and went door to door, asking if anyone wanted to buy a Chrysler car. The second door he knocked on, he found someone who said yes. Now, it was Friday, and the customer said he had to go to the bank and get financing. Long story short, Gerry spent the day waiting for what would be a no, and no one called in asking about the car from our radio advertisement.

The next day, we said goodbye to Mitzi and sat around making contingency plans. On Sunday, we decided to play golf on what was the farthest northern golf course in the United States. We only played nine holes before the snowstorm got the better of us, but we did get the certificate! Sitting in the clubhouse having a couple of hot buttered rums to warm up, a group of four men came in. They were very dirty and quite drunk. Gerry started up a conversation with them. They asked us why we were in Fairbanks and told us they were returning after a five-day hunting trip. When Gerry told them that we were selling the car we arrived in, the drunkest and dirtiest asked what kind of car it was. Gerry told him it was a Chrysler, and he said he was interested in a Chrysler for his wife. Gerry took him out to look at it and he said he'd take it for cash and gave Gerry a $500 deposit. Gerry told him what hotel we were staying in and arranged for the man to meet us at the hotel at 10am the next day. We left and decided if the man did not show up the next morning, we would keep his deposit and put the Chrysler on consignment with the Chrysler dealer.

The next morning, just as we were getting ready to take the car to the Chrysler dealer, having no anticipation that the man would show up, let alone remember the deal, there was a knock on the door. I opened it to a gentleman in a three-piece pin-striped suit, accompanied by another gentleman carrying a briefcase. The first gentleman introduced himself as the man we had met in the bar the day before and introduced the other man as his lawyer. Seemed he was the GMC dealer in town, but his wife wanted a Chrysler and Gerry's was a good deal. The lawyer made sure all the paperwork was in order and we were who we said we were. Money was exchanged, we all shook hands, and that's how the car business was conducted in Alaska!

Back To Vietnam

As a result of the loss to my father on the golf course and in the hopes of one day beating him, we decided to join the Saigon golf club. The course was a bit different than most golf courses, in that along two of its fairways were active mine fields and on one of its greens, there was a 'dog trap.' Living next to the green was a Vietnamese family with a little dog that was trained to fetch golf balls and drop them into the mine field. The papa san, or grandfather of the family, knew where the mines were planted. He would then retrieve the balls and sell them back to the golfers. One day, Gerry was golfing with Chuck. When he teed off on this particular hole, sure enough, the little dog came running out and picked up his ball. Gerry, refusing to be shaken down by the dog, ran down the fairway, yelling and shaking his club. This scared the dog, disorienting him. Instead of running towards the trap, he ran to the green and dropped his ball into the hole, giving Gerry a hole in one! Chuck began laughing and said Gerry either had just made a deal with the devil or was God. In the retelling of this story, Chuck forgot about the devil option and started calling Gerry 'God.' I made the mistake of commenting that, if he was God, I must be the Virgin Mary, which prompted Chuck to call us God and Mary.

Despite the war, living in Saigon was a life of affluence. We were members of the yacht club, the sports club (tennis), and the golf club. We were privileged to sit courtside at an exhibition between Bai, the

72

tennis pro at our club, and Arthur Ashe. We also had the opportunity to watch Arthur Ashe and Ron Laver play doubles against Bai and his assistant. We were getting paid more than we could spend and had many opportunities to travel to many of the exotic spots in Asia. The food—a combination of French, Vietnamese, and Chinese—was to die for. My brother Tony was hired by Chrysler Military Sales to work in Thailand and Okinawa. My parents, Gerry's mother, my brothers Michael and Joe, and my sister Azalia all visited us in either Thailand and/or Vietnam.

But Saigon was not without its dangers. Chuck and Joanne had three children—Johnny, 10; Jay, seven; and Julie, five—and they were beginning to think that the children would be better off living in the States. About this time, one of their maids, while shopping in the central market, saw another of the maids with Julie, their little daughter. Getting suspicious, the maid called the joint Vietnamese American patrol, who questioned the maid and took Julie home. This was the straw that broke the camel's back so to speak, as it was suspected that the maid had intended to sell Julie, and it was arranged that the three children would be sent back to the States to live with their grandparents in California. They were accompanied by their uncle, Terry, who also arranged for the children to attend a boarding school five days a week and stay with their grandparents on the weekends.

This arrangement almost fell apart when, one day, the children were attending Bible class (the school was Catholic—the children were not). The subject was the Baltimore Catechism. I'm sure all you Catholics remember the first page of the Catechism: Who is God? Where is God? Is God good?

Well, when the question came up about where God is, little Jay started waving his hand wildly. When the nun called upon him, he blurted out, "God is in Saigon, and his mother, Mary, is there too!"

After several letters and tapes back and forth between California and Saigon, I can only speculate on the explanation! The children were permitted to stay both at school and at their grandparents.

By mid-1972, peace talks between North Vietnam and the United States, in the persons of Le Duc Tho and Henry Kissinger, began and the light at the end of the tunnel seemed to be around the corner. Ironically, the end came for me about the same way my introduction to the country came about.

One night, at about 10pm, while we were lying in bed, we heard a horrific explosion followed by the plastic, which covered our bedroom window, moving into our bedroom and then out again. Glass didn't survive the B-52 bombings. Gerry told me we experienced an implosion. Our apartment was on the second floor. So, we ran out into the hallway and raced up the stairs to the roof on the sixth floor to see what was happening, as smaller explosions rattled the building. What we saw was the whole horizon of Saigon ablaze.

Back in our apartment, I called Military Assistance Command to find out what was happening. I was told to not worry, Saigon was not under attack, the US military had the situation in hand. The cause of the explosions? The friendlies, in the form of the Vietnamese army, had located a Viet Kong cache of armaments within the city of Saigon and to get rid of them piled them in one huge pile and detonated it!

The peace talks were making progress. Gerry was already sending his salesmen to other posts in Asia or home, as the bases were closing one by one. The PX personnel were initiating deactivation plans for their stores. We decided that enough was enough. Gerry had already been given the territory of Thailand, Guam, and the Philippines, along with Vietnam, Cambodia, and Laos and it was felt that all of SE Asia could be handled by the Thailand office. The next morning, Gerry booked a ticket to Bangkok to look for a place for us to live. Since my office had a helipad on the roof, we decided that whatever happened, I had a way of getting out of Saigon in a hurry, so I remained in Saigon to pack up our possessions and mail them to Bangkok. By remaining, I was also able to help the commander I worked for deactivate our office.

Since I was in a position to know, various people were asking me the timeline of the deactivation of the bases throughout Vietnam. My answer was always, "If I told you, I would have to kill you!"

During this time, my mother had written me a letter, asking me if I had ever met my aunt's ex-husband, who was supposedly in Vietnam selling cars. When I asked Gerry if he knew this ex-uncle of mine, he replied he did, and so did I.

He reminded me that although we did not know it at the time, the man he introduced me to at the PX in Taiwan four years before was my ex-uncle, Bob. Because of my position the last few weeks of my stay in Saigon, I re-met the man when he came up to my office trying to get information out of me. I informed him that if I told him I would have to kill him!

THAILAND

At the end of February 1973, we officially moved to Thailand. My parents were quite distressed at this move because they could not find the country on our family atlas. They were much relieved to hear that Thailand used to be called Siam. Gerry's mother was OK with the move since she had already visited the country in 1969 when we toured Asia on a Harles family vacation.

While the bungalow Gerry had found for us was being readied, we stayed in the Dusit Thani Hotel. By the time I arrived in Bangkok, Gerry had been in the hotel for a week, and knew all the 'good' restaurants to go to dinner. On my first night, he took me to the Normandie Grill in the Oriental Hotel with our friend John. He flew for Air America and was also staying at the same hotel. The Oriental Hotel was one of the oldest hotels in Bangkok, plus it had Bangkok's only five-star restaurant.

Since I read all the tourist books when I visit a country, I told Gerry and John that they wouldn't get in the restaurant without a suit coat and tie, even with reservations. A discussion ensued, and they finally acquiesced to wearing suit coats. Upon arrival at the restaurant, the host politely told them they needed ties to dine. When they explained that they did not have any, the host told them to not worry. He had ties for them and promptly supplied each of them with a string tie. This started the evening on a rather raucous note as the string ties looked ridiculous on them. As we were having our first course, two men walked into the restaurant in almost identical seersucker suits, and string ties.

As they passed our table, Gerry commented, "Do you suppose they arrived without clothes and the host supplied them with both suits and ties?" We roared with laughter at the comment… Well, you had to be there… on your second martini!

The second night, Gerry told me we were going to eat at the only English pub in Bangkok. When we pulled into the parking lot, behind the restaurant, there was an old lady squatting down, cooking something on a little hibachi. Gerry pointed her out and told me to remember her. We entered the pub, and I must admit it took me back to England, including the mugs of beer and the dart board on the wall. We ordered meat pies, and the waiter left through a door that had a 'Do Not Enter' sign on it.

Gerry pointed to the door and said, "Guess where that door leads?"
I asked, "Where?"
He told me, "The parking lot!"

It seemed the parking lot was the kitchen, and the mamma san squatting over the hibachi was the chef! I thought, *Welcome to Asia*.

Compared to Saigon, Bangkok was a tame city as far as the war was concerned. There was even a store called Design Thai, where you could buy ready-made dresses, and a supermarket called Kangaroo that had foods like Whole Foods. When we moved to the United States, I actually found a store in Sarasota, Florida, called Design Thai, which was in fact associated with the store in Bangkok! Small world!

At that time, when you lived in Asia, it really was necessary to have help with the housework. Washing clothes without a washing machine was a challenge, and as I was working 8–10 hours each day, getting dinner on the table in the evening was impossible. Consequently, we needed to find someone to fill this position.

Our friends Jack and Catherine, who had come to Bangkok a couple of years earlier, suggested the Women's Exchange, which was an unofficial placement service for English-speaking individuals needing help. I asked Gerry to go and find us someone, since he was more experienced at judging people.

He wasn't too excited at the prospect, but he went, and he told me later, "I went with a bad attitude and when I got there, there were several women seeking employment. One lady was squatting on her haunches with a frown on her face. She looked like I felt, and something made me start talking to her. When I asked her if she had any references, she gave me a four-page letter from her previous employers explaining her qualifications.

"The letter told me that she had worked for 20 years for her former employers, the Dunkins, and the only reason she was unemployed was because they had moved to Rangoon, the capital of Burma (now called Myanmar). The Burmese and the Thais do not get along, so they could not bring her."

Gerry bought her home to get my approval, and that is how I met Ahp, the best cook and housekeeper I ever had. Not only that, but all of Bangkok, it seemed, had heard of Ahp, as the Dunkins were quite prominent in the foreign community and did a lot of entertaining. But more important, Ahp and I thought alike; she put things right where I thought they should go, making my world a lot easier!

We had been in Bangkok about eight months when I got involved in the Women's Club. Jack and Catherine had become good friends, and Catherine was the president. Once a year, the Women's Club put on an affair called Table Wonderland. Every country was represented, 'menus' were given to the attendees, and it was attended by the who's who in Bangkok. The affair was held on the king's palace grounds and the unofficial head of the planning committee was the king's sister. I was on the committee as the marketing person, writing an advertisement for the affair and printing the 'menu.'

At this same time, Chrysler Military Sales took on the sale of Harley-Davidson motorcycles along with the Chrysler, Plymouth, and

Dodges they sold to the military. The week before I was having the Table Planning Committee meet at my house, an event the king's sister was going to attend, Gerry took the Harley-Davidson down south to Utapao AFB to spend a day with his salesman.

We had words before Gerry left. He was probably driving too fast because of our argument, and somehow, a bus loaded with people ran him off the road and into a rice paddy. He found himself laying in the paddy unhurt and thanking his lucky stars, when the motorcycle he had been thrown from came down on his leg. The bus had stopped when the driver realized he had run Gerry off the road and several of the occupants ran into the rice paddy and pulled the motorcycle off him and him out of the rice paddy.

The motorcycle was none the worse for wear, so Gerry thanked his helpers, got back on the motorcycle, and continued his trip. He took care of his business, covered in mud from the paddy, and proceeded to Pattaya Beach to check into his hotel. By that time, his leg was aching, and his instincts told him not to take his boot off. He called me and told me he had been in an accident and hurt his leg. Since it was only 4:30, I told him to check out of the hotel and come home.

When he got home, he took off his muddy clothes and his boots. Although his blue jeans were not ripped, nor was the boot scuffed, he had a 3-inch gash on his shinbone that was so deep, the bone was exposed. I insisted he go to the hospital and have the wound looked at, but he refused. The next day, I could see he was in pain, and I knew he should go to the hospital; he again refused. As I left for work, I said goodbye and told him if he died from that wound, I had enjoyed our life up to that point.

When Ahp came to work that day, she took one look at his leg and browbeat him until he drove himself to the hospital. The doctor he saw stitched up the wound and applied a cloth-like cast on his leg. When I got home that night, he was still in pain, but we thought he would be okay in time. The next morning, he was still in pain and letting me know constantly. I was glad Ahp would take care of him and I could go to work.

Three days later, Gerry was still in pain and his leg had started swelling. When Ahp came to work, she insisted he take off the cast. Gerry relayed that when the cast came off, Ahp grabbed his leg and started massaging it. She told him his leg was filled with "wind" and he might lose it. This got Gerry's attention, and he called me and put Ahp on the telephone. From what she was explaining to me, I concluded that she was talking about gangrene and told Gerry to go to the hospital immediately. I called the hospital and asked to speak to a doctor that spoke English. To explain, because Gerry didn't have US military credentials, he could not go to the American hospital, so he went to the Thai hospital. I spoke to the doctor, who did not treat Gerry's leg originally, and said he would take care of him when he arrived.

The doctor called after Gerry left and told me that the wound had never been cleaned out on Gerry's first visit, and that Ahp massaging his leg and getting him to the hospital had probably saved his leg. He also told me that the wound would heal better if it had a skin graft over it. If we agreed, he could schedule it for the next day, which was a Friday. I told the doctor to schedule it and I would have Gerry at the hospital at 4am on Friday.

After much discussion, Gerry agreed the skin graft would be the best solution for getting his leg back in shape the fastest and I drove him to the hospital on Friday morning. By Friday afternoon, Gerry's operation was over, and he was conscious and checked into a room for a two-day stay. I went to visit him, and he was not in the best frame of mind. Let me digress and explain my theory about men, women, and pain. In my opinion, the Y chromosome that is inherent in men makes them all babies when it comes to pain. They can't just lay there sick or in pain; they must tell you about it every minute! It is for this reason that nature made it so that men don't have babies! So, it was with relief when I kissed Gerry goodbye and went home.

Now, this was the very weekend I was having the Table Planning Committee over to my house for a planning session. So, I was happy that Gerry was in the hospital and out of my hair when the ladies arrived. But when I arrived home from the hospital, Gerry called me and started complaining that his room was hot; he thought they had given him a room without air conditioning. (Remember, Bangkok is on the equator, so air conditioning is a necessity.)

Apparently, he was right because they moved him to another room, which he called to tell me was somewhat better. As I was awaiting my guests to arrive, I received a telephone call from the doctor. He reported on the operation, and then very diplomatically, asked me to please come and pick up Gerry. He told me, as his wife, I could handle him better than the nurses in the hospital! I told him I could not pick him up until later that afternoon as I was having a very important meeting. His reply was he understood but to please hurry!

There was a funny story as a result of Gerry's accident. Jack and Catherine, as representatives of the American Chamber of Commerce, were invited to a formal cocktail party with the representatives of the foreign businesses in Bangkok. Since Gerry was out of commission, they suggested that I accompany their visiting son-in-law, Patrick. Patrick worked for Berliet, a heavy-duty truck company headquartered in France. This was Patrick, our friend from Vietnam. Of course, I accepted. We didn't know anyone, so we took delight in introducing ourselves as Patrick, the truck salesman, and Judy, the car salesman!

We played a lot of golf in Thailand. It was so much more fun because we had found that Jack and Catherine enjoyed the game as much as we did. There was one golf course in Bangkok that we played frequently because the Thais thought it was haunted. The course had been designed by Robert Trent Jones, who designed it in yards, but by mistake, it was laid out in meters. So, the par 3s played like par 4s and par 4s, well, you get the picture. We would usually get up early on Saturdays and get to the course before sunrise, which was 7am. We were usually the first four-some to tee off. One day, we arrived around 6:45

and there was already eight people on the first tee. The group had a reputation for playing very slow golf. As the sun came up, Gerry confidently swaggered up to the group and said, "Mind if we play through," and teed off!

Speaking of golf, one day, we were behind a group, which consisted of eight golfers, eight caddies, and four forecaddies. It looked like an army on the course. As we approached the ninth tee, which brought us back to the beginning of the golf course, Gerry went over to the starter and asked how he could let the group tee off. As Gerry pointed out, there were eight people golfing. The starter looked at him and with a straight face said, "Oh no, sir. That's two foursomes!"

Bangkok is not known for its beaches. True, it is on the Chao Phraya River, but to really get to a beach with sand and swimmable water, you must go to either Pattaya Beach, which is a famous vacation site, or any small town on the Gulf of Siam. We spent one Sunday playing golf in the morning and going to one of these small towns for the beach in the afternoon. When we got to the beach, we set up a picnic blanket and started enjoying the day. We had all sorts of vendors come to try to sell us their wares, including one who sold cold beer and oysters. We were enjoying the fare, along with haggling for a few souvenirs, when I noticed that my engagement ring had fallen off my finger. We started looking in the sand, and when we attracted a crowd, Gerry offered a reward to anyone who found the ring.

After about 45 minutes when I was getting flustered at the thought of losing my ring, an old lady approached and asked the group what they were looking for. Someone told her a diamond ring and added that there was a reward for finding it. The old lady stooped down and grabbed a handful of sand, opened her hand, and my ring was in her palm! Gerry gave her the reward, which was equivalent to $20, and a big hug. Everyone clapped and started breaking up. To this day, I'll never know if it was the luck of the grab or the powers the crowd said she had.

LAOS

One long weekend, we decided to go to Laos. Gerry went ahead of me on some business on Thursday and I followed on Friday. I don't know how much business he did do. He called me from the hotel's pool to tell me he had arrived, and that the hotel was very nice (which meant it had air conditioning and a restaurant).

He told me that, besides himself, there were two men that he suspected were KGB. When I asked him why, he told me that they went everywhere together, even to the pool's bathroom, and did not reply to any of his advances to get acquainted. To cap it all off, they had identical swimming suits! He speculated they must have bought them at the Russian PX! Well, Laos did have a reputation at that time (1973 to 1975) of being the spy capital of Southeast Asia, so maybe they were indeed KGB.

When I arrived, Gerry told me we had been invited to lunch by Don and Mickie, who were friends of ours from Vietnam. Remember the incident where we were never served dinner, just drinks? Hoping this time we were going to get something to eat, we were not disappointed. Don entertained us with his gun collection. What interested us the most was a gun hand made by the Muong, who were the tribal people in Laos helping the US in information gathering and fire-power against the Viet Cong. Don said he could get one of these guns anytime because he had contacts among the Muong and he gave Gerry the gun. I actually carried this through customs in Thailand when we returned from Laos, and to prove to the customs official that the gun could not be fired, I described it as an old time flint lock like the ones used in our revolutionary war. Fortunately, the official was as ignorant as myself because, in the car going home, Gerry told me I actually had described how the gun worked! I still have that gun today but I never carried it through customs again!

That evening, we went to the White Rose Bar. I had read that it was a gathering place for spies! Well, if we met any, we weren't aware of it. There was a poster on the wall of President Richard Nixon with the caption, "Would you buy a used car from this man?" (Remember this was during Watergate). Gerry being a car salesman and Canadian couldn't understand what was so funny. In the explanation, it didn't seem that funny to me either.

On Saturday evening, after a great dinner, we ended up in our hotel bar, where we met two very interesting men. One was a writer for an Italian newspaper, which, as he was proud to say, had 'communist leanings.' The other was a Japanese-American who told us he was sent over to Asia to 'work' for the army, whatever that meant. The conversation between Gerry and these two men was very interesting. Basically, it was our side of the Vietnam War as opposed to the other side. We, at the end of the evening, parted as friends. It was a short, but very interesting trip.

Family In Asia

While we were living in Asia, as I mentioned earlier, I was fortunate to have two of my brothers, my sister, and my parents visit me. In addition, Tony worked in both Thailand and Okinawa for Chrysler. Each one had memorable experiences while visiting and could tell many stories about their visits, but the three that really stand out was taking Michael to Burma, Azalia to Cambodia, and Joe just hanging with Gerry!

Michael was a pilot, and when we flew into Rangoon, as we approached the runway, we hit what's called a shear factor. The plane tipped one wing up before the pilot leveled it and landed. Everyone clapped and marveled at the way the pilot 'dipped' the plane.

When I looked at Michael, he was sheet white and shaking. I jokingly said to him, "What's the matter? You don't like the landing?"

He looked at me and said, "We're lucky to be alive." Sober thought and a bad start to our Burmese vacation.

After spending the rest of the day touring Rangoon, we checked into the Inya Lake Hotel, which was one of the best hotels for foreigners in Rangoon. After dinner, Michael, Gerry, and I ended up on the top terrace of the hotel with the tour guide who I think had a thing for Michael. We spent several hours talking and drinking, until finally, the waiter came and told us the terrace bar was closing. Gerry ordered one last drink, but the waiter said he had no more water or ice (Gerry was drinking scotch and water, the bar having run out of tonic for gin and tonics earlier). Gerry in his insistent way looked at the waiter and said, "I'm sure you can come up with some water from somewhere!"

We kept on talking. Michael got my attention and motioned to the side of the terrace, where the waiter had a bucket on a rope, that he was dipping into the river. An unlimited supply of water. It landed as number two on Michael's list of 'Burma is interesting' for the folks back home! The following day, we flew to Pagan, with no untoward instances to add to Michael's list.

We toured Pagan, one of the richest archaeological sites in Asia. That night, our hotel had plenty of water, ice, and tonic which we enjoyed with no story worthy incidents.

The following day, we flew to Mandalay and took a bus tour of the city. Our first stop was Mandalay Hill. The tour guide told us that the view on the top was worth the climb, but to be fair, she told us that there was a little over 2,000 steps, and it would take over two hours! One of the German tourists stood up and, in German, remarked that we should vote on whether we wanted to stop. Gerry stood up and, in German, pointed out that this was not a democracy but a tour bus. The tour guide solved the problem by saying those who wanted to stay could get off and the bus would return in two hours to pick them up. Michael, Gerry, and I got off, along with two young men from France and two ladies from Mexico. The climb was tiring, but the view was worth it! Of the seven of us, only five of us made it to the top, but I must admit, since Mandalay is a very flat city, even halfway up, the view was spectacular.

The bus picked us up around noon, and the driver told us he was taking us to a monastery to have lunch; the others were already there. On the way, Gerry told the driver that we were looking for a Buddha statue for our house and asked where the best place to buy one was. The driver told us the best place to purchase one was under the Maha Myat Muni Pagoda, but the tour had already visited this site. Gerry asked the driver if, for some renumeration, he would take us to this site after stopping for lunch. He told us there was not enough time. When he stopped at the monastery where we were having lunch, we waited for the others to get off the bus and then asked the driver to take us to the pagoda. This was probably the highlight of the tour. The 'basement' of the pagoda was a sight to see. On top were hundreds of handicraft shops, but underneath were almost as many doing nothing but carving and painting Buddha statues. We purchased one of the Buddhas painted gold, and Michael added hi-jacking a bus to his list of 'Burma is interesting.' We then rejoined the tour with our bus in time to get to the airport to fly back to Rangoon.

When we were getting ready to leave the tour, the tour guide told us that, theoretically, it was illegal to take Buddhas out of the country, so when we departed the following day, we put a sock over the statue, put it in the backpack with our camera equipment, and made Michael carry it out. Since he was taller than most Burmese, we figured they wouldn't be able to see what was poking out of the backpack! Thus, adding smuggling a Buddha out of the country to his 'Burma is interesting' list.

We still have that Buddha to this day. It has sat in a prominent place in every home we have lived in. A golden Buddha statue with a black nose, obtained from the sock that was put over its head for its departure from Burma!

Visiting Thailand was a wonderful experience for my family but staying in Thailand was another experience in itself. It was almost impossible to obtain a permanent visa, unless you were in the diplomatic core, or willing to bribe someone. Even Jack, who was president of the American Chamber of Commerce, and refused to pay any bribes, was 'dragged off' to jail about every four months in the hopes that the US Embassy would pay up before they demanded that he be released! For Chrysler Military Sales, Gerry had two choices. He could either send his agents out of the country every month, or he could hire someone to take care of the problem. When the first option didn't work (the agents treated the trip as a vacation and stayed longer than the two days necessary to solve the problem), Gerry hired Peter. Peter was given all the passports, including mine and Gerry's, and the passports went in and out of the country every month.

When my younger brother and sister Joe and Azalia were coming to visit me in Thailand, I told my parents to get each of them two 30-day visas. After quite a bit of aggravation, numerous trips to Chicago to the Thai Consulate, and $200, the mission was accomplished. We entertained the two of them with tours, trips to Pattaya Beach, and a sailing trip around Guam at the start of their vacation. They even got to celebrate the Fourth of July with every American in Bangkok, at the polo club, complete with lots of security and secret service types guarding the perimeter! But with all this and more, Joe decided to go home after 30 days; he missed his girlfriend. Azalia on the other hand was excited about staying another 30 days.

When we asked the American Consulate how we were supposed to activate that second 30-day visa, we were told we needed to get a bond at our bank and the bank would know how to proceed. We went to the bank and gave the task to our banker, who told us that a bond was worthless. The Thais wouldn't honor it and all that would happen was we would lose the cost of the bond, and the Thais would be alerted to the fact that that there was an individual who was in the country without a visa. However, we did need to activate the visa so Azalia could leave the country.

So, we contacted our 'friend' Peter, and he arranged for me and Azalia to take a taxi to the Thai-Cambodian border. He told us all we had to do was walk across the bridge, thus leaving Thailand, and entering Cambodia, where American's didn't need a visa, get a Cambodian entry stamp, turn around and leave Cambodia, thus getting a Cambodian exit stamp, cross the bridge again and have Azalia's and my passports stamped with an entry stamp. Simple, except for the wild 100-mile, non-air-conditioned taxi ride with what we thought was a driver who was either drunk or feeling the morning after effects, coupled with the nervousness of brazenly thumbing our noses at both countries' systems. Arriving at the border, we did what we were told to do, even taking a few pictures of the border that closed shortly after our adventure, and joyously found out that we were going to go back with a new driver in a car with air conditioning!

Now, Joe had the experience of taking public transportation in Bangkok. It started when Gerry was stuck with two cars at the office. His boss, Arnold, had driven one and then left it at the office when he flew to Japan. Gerry called and asked if Joe knew how to drive. Joe was 16, so of course, he could drive but picking up that extra car meant he had to drive an American car on the left-hand side of the road. Joe said he could do it, so Ahp went out to the street and hailed an open-air taxi. We put Joe in the taxi and Ahp told the driver where to go.

Well, Joe made it to the office and back home with no problem. But he told us, first the driver asked him if he wanted to change money, then asked him if he wanted any drugs (it was easy to get heroin in Thailand, but he also offered marijuana). When Joe said no to both, the driver asked him if he wanted a girl, then in exasperation, he asked Joe if he wanted a boy! Joe said he was lucky that, right about then, they arrived at the office. He was afraid of what the man was going to offer him next!

Joe also had the pleasure (or experience, whichever way you hear the story) of spending Bastille Day with Gerry and Patrick. The celebration consisted of drinking all day by the pool, and then going to one of the many steam rooms, where I imagine, Joe was subjected to many of the same questions the taxi driver had asked him. But the worse part in my mind was when Gerry came home at 1am, without Joe. When I asked him where Joe was, he told me they had left him in one of the steam rooms. As I am loudly yelling, "Left him? He's only 16 and doesn't have any money!" There was a knock at the door and there was Joe asking me to pay his taxi driver.

As I mentioned, Peter took care of our passports. When we had to leave Thailand, he delivered the passports with all the necessary paperwork taken care of that kept us legally in the country and allowed us to leave. Just before Saigon fell, Gerry and I made one more visit to Vietnam. When we got to the customs desk at the airport, the official kept asking me something I did not understand, except for the fact that he was not letting me get on the plane. When a translator arrived, I understood that the official wanted to know from which country did I enter Thailand so he could give me the correct exit papers. Well, I hadn't a clue where I came from, Peter took care of all that. Finally, I was given a paper that said I came from Laos and the problem was averted. When I returned to Thailand, I told Peter that the next time I left Thailand he needed to tell me where I came from. I meant which country, but the next time I left Thailand, Peter not only told me from which country I came, but he drew a map of the border crossing, with its name and hours of operation!

NEPAL

In 1974, America experienced a fuel crisis. There were pictures of long lines at gas stations, and the sales of new cars dropped drastically. Because we were in the business of selling cars, Gerry spent 250 days traveling to all the bases in Guam, the Philippines, Vietnam, Laos, Cambodia, and of course, Thailand.

Consequently, I was left in Thailand to tend the home fires. But the truth was, I also wanted to travel; so, the other 100 days Gerry was not traveling for Chrysler, he was going on trips with me. Burma was one such trip we took with Michael, another was Nepal.

I always joke that I spent four years in Asia and never got the chance to visit India, which was my destination back in 1967 when I met Gerry on that boat! But I did have the opportunity to see the country from across the Sarda River when I was touring Nepal. We spent three days seeing all the sights in Kathmandu, including the Kali Festival, and what was to become the last living goddess.

Gerry always took slides of all our adventures. For the Kali Festival, where they killed a fattened goat, he climbed up a wall to take pictures. He told me to stand back in case the blood splattered, unlike the more aggressive tourists (whose nationality shall remain nameless), who crowded right up to the ceremonial altar. Well, there was splattering, and I was glad that I had observed the ceremony from afar, and Gerry got some interesting pictures, including some of shocked blood splattered tourists!

The living goddess had an interesting story. The present goddess was around 12 years old. She was chosen when she was a baby under one. She was put in a darkened pagoda with all the babies of that age whose parents were from the goldsmith profession. The babies were then subjected to loud noises and the baby who did not cry was deemed the goddess. The goddess 'ruled' until she menstruated and then she was sent back to her family and another goddess was chosen. According to National Geographic, this goddess was the last goddess because it was deemed to be child abuse and the custom was abandoned, mainly because the goddess had no real life after her tenure was over. No one wanted to marry her, and she became an outcast to the society that had worshipped her in her youth!

The second part of our trip was to Tiger Tops, a resort situated in one of Nepal's national parks. We flew to the resort on a small plane out of Kathmandu and landed on a single runway in the middle of the jungle. The runway was lined on either side with people, who had come from the nearby village just to see the tourists. Upon leaving the plane, we were given the option of proceeding to Tiger Tops on either an elephant or by jeep. We were cautioned, however, that there was only one jeep, which held four people plus the driver, so if more than four people opted for the jeep, there would be a wait.

Well, our decision was an immediate elephant. So, Gerry and I got on one and took off. When we arrived at the resort, we saw that the hotel was built into trees. The doors to the rooms were elephant high, so you did not have to get down off the elephant, but just had to step over to your hotel room! We were told that dinner would be at seven, but drinks and appetizers would be served at six in the main lodge, which was at ground level. By the way, there were also stairs to the rooms. At six, we went to the lodge and were greeted by the park's resident park director, who was American. Gerry asked him what brought him to Nepal, and he told us he met his wife in college. She was majoring in animal husbandry, and he was going to be a veterinarian, and coincidentally, she was Nepalese. So, he asked for and obtained the position when both were ready to start their careers. He told us that he was very impressed with me, because I had 'dressed for dinner.' I had on an elegant long skirt and silk top and, back in those days, went everywhere with my jewelry. He said the last person who 'dressed for dinner' was Jacqueline Kennedy when she had visited. Wow! Jacqueline Kennedy was one of my heroines at the time.

I will always remember that compliment. However, the evening went downhill from there. We were told that the resort had baited a section of the jungle, visible from the lodge, in the hopes that a hungry tiger would come for us to observe how Tiger Tops got its name. So, after dinner, the whole tour group got together for an after-dinner drink, got to know each other, and generally had a pleasant evening while waiting for a signal that a tiger was feeding. As it got later and later, people started saying goodnight and going to their rooms, until all that was left was me, Gerry, and the young tour guide. The tiger still had not come, and I said my goodnight and went off to bed.

I don't know what time it was when Gerry came to bed, but the next morning, he told me that after I left, the tour guide offered him some marijuana which he said would enhance the experience. But Gerry said he did not know what the whole marijuana thing was all about. He did not feel a thing! I told him that he would not have known the difference with all the liquor he had consumed!

The next day, we went camera hunting on elephants. The most exciting thing we came across was a herd of rhinos. To this day, I cannot remember if they were white or black. What I do remember is the way the elephant drivers managed to gather them in a circle so we could take pictures. Suddenly, one of the rhinos, to protect her baby, charged out of the circle.

Unfortunately, she charged our elephant, who reared up on his hind legs to chase her away. Gerry gave me his camera and yelled, "Take a picture!"

Holding on for dear life, I snarled back, "If you want a picture, you take it!"

Well, we did get some great pictures, just not any of a charging rhino!

BACK IN THAILAND

Thailand's currency is the baht. When we lived there, one US dollar was equivalent to 20 baht. We dealt with the Chase Manhattan Bank, where we could have both a dollar and a baht account. To obtain baht, all we had to do was write a dollar check. Gerry had had a Chase account since 1967 when he went to work for Chrysler Military Sales, as that was where his commissions were deposited. However, in the move from Vietnam to Thailand, he had misplaced his last book of checks. So, he went to the Chase Bank in Bangkok and ordered more checks. After a month, his checks had not arrived, and he demanded to see the manager of the bank.

That is how we met Chachival Lobek. Chachival told Gerry he would expedite the checks. When another month went by and still no checks, Gerry went back to complain again and Chachival told him he would put a tracer on the checks, but in the meantime, when he needed funds, he could come to him, and he would authorize Gerry's transactions without checks. Gerry began calling Chachival his father, since he had to ask him for funds!

As mentioned earlier, our best friends in Bangkok were Jack and Catherine. They entertained most of the visiting VIPs, especially those dealing with Thai/American business, with Jack being president of the American Chamber of Commerce. One Friday, Jack called Gerry about the Sunday golf game and mentioned the fact that they were entertaining David Rockefeller, the president of Chase Manhattan Bank, and they had not invited us because Jack did not want a confrontation about Gerry's check situation. Gerry said he understood.

On Saturday, we went to the bank to get the funds we needed to run the household and the office, and while I wrote the checks we needed and deposited the deposits from the car sales that week, Gerry went over to chat with Chachival and have him authorize a withdrawal of cash for his upcoming business trip to the Philippines. As he was sitting there, Chachival rigidly stood and said, "Good day Mr. Rockefeller." When Gerry turned around, Chachival introduced him to David Rockefeller. Gerry stood and they shook hands. Chachival said, "Mr. Harles is one of our best customers!"

David Rockefeller said, "Glad to meet you, Mr. Harles. Is there anything our bank can do for you?"

Well, not to bore you, let's just say that the story of the checks was discussed. Two things came from this encounter besides Gerry having met David Rockefeller. One: within a week, we were sent 500 checks. Two: Gerry received a call from Jack Scott that started out with, "You bastard…" The rest of the call was never discussed.

INDONESIA

In 1974, we decided to go to Indonesia for Christmas. The trip started off at Jack and Catherine's house the night before, when we went to a dinner party. It was special because Gerry had just returned from a business trip to the Philippines, and our French friend, Patrick, was visiting his in-laws, Jack and Catherine. After dinner and after-dinner drinks, Gerry wanted to leave as we had to get up early in the morning for the flight to Indonesia. For once, I was the one who wanted to stay, as one of the guests had gone to Kodaikanal in India, with Kathy, Patrick's wife and Jack and Catherine's daughter. I was questioning him about India and what it was like to grow up there. So, we stayed too late, had one too many drinks, and went to bed very late.

In the morning, we finished packing and called a taxi. We were what I call 'rocky,' not quite sober, but not drunk! In the taxi, Gerry pulled out a split of Champagne and said he got it from the airline to celebrate the start of our trip. I said that was a good idea, so Gerry popped the cork, and with the pop, the taxi driver thought something was wrong and jerked the steering wheel, driving the taxi into a stone wall (the road we were on was very narrow)! Well, he backed away from the wall and kept driving to the airport; he didn't even acknowledge that perhaps we had made the sound!

When we got to the airport and checked in, we were told that the flight had been delayed. So, we went to the VIP lounge to wait it out.

(Side note: because Gerry was traveling so much, he had a VIP card for every airline in existence at the time.) Lucky us, because it was the Christmas holiday, the lounge was serving complimentary Champagne! Two hours later, they finally called our flight.

As if we needed it, the flight was serving complimentary drinks, so since I had never tasted Genever, the Dutch gin, Gerry ordered us each a glass. To this day, and I owned a liquor store for 33 years, every time I have tasted Genever, I have come to the same conclusion: it is awful. So, I held the glass, minus one sip, until the stewardess cleared the drinks for take-off. Gerry, on the other hand, managed to get two or three glasses down before we took off.

By the time we arrived in Djakarta, Gerry had passed the 'rocky' point, and I was frankly angry with him. We had to claim our bags, go through customs, and wait with our bags until the flight that was taking us to Bali, where we were spending a week, was called. With the more than two-hour layover, we intended to call a friend of ours from Saigon, Don, who had been assigned to Djakarta on some UN project. Unfortunately, Don and his family had gone to the States for the Christmas holiday.

Since we had nothing to do but wait, I pulled out a book, and gave Gerry one of the magazines he had brought. He gave the magazine back to me and told me he would be right back. When the flight was called for check-in, I looked around for Gerry, and not seeing him, I decided to wait till the last minute to check in. Well, the last minute came and went and still no Gerry. I had even had him paged. So, here was my dilemma: I had both passports and all our bags, but no money, and Gerry had plenty of money but no clothes or passport!

As they were closing the airport, I decided to call a taxi, loaded all our bags, and told the driver to take me to the Hotel Indonesia, the best hotel in town. When we arrived at the hotel, I went to the reception desk and told them I had no Indonesian money, asked them to please pay the taxi driver, including an appropriate tip, and put it on my bill. They said that was no problem. So, with my American Express card, I checked in. They always say, "Never go anywhere without it!"

The next morning, I decided to call Armando, our friend in Bangkok with 'connections,' but for the life of me, I could not remember his telephone number. I remembered all the numbers, but I couldn't remember in what order. So, I spent a couple of hours trying to place a call, which took about 30 minutes, each time putting the numbers in a different order. Giving up, I went down to the restaurant and had lunch, walked around the hotel for a bit, ending up in the bar, where I ordered a scotch and water, and an extra glass of water. Nursing my drink, I pondered life without Gerry, and decided I really didn't want my life without Gerry. I was on my third drink when I suddenly heard, "Judy Vignocchi Harles, please pick up phone number one."

When I picked up the phone, lo and behold, it was Gerry! He asked me where I was and when I told him the Hotel Indonesia, he told me he was also there. He told me what room he was in and asked me to come up to his room. Well, finding his room was quite an adventure. He was on the fourth floor, which was partially under renovation, down a hallway with no carpet, only bare flooring. His room was outdated and not at all up to Hotel Indonesia standards! My comment was, "Seems you got the ha-ha room. So, this is where they put drunks who arrive with money but no passports." We said our 'I'm sorrys,' and then Gerry checked out of his room and into mine.

We went out for a great dinner, the topic of discussion was how Gerry was going to get an Indonesian stamp in his passport, since he had disappeared before he got one and for all intents and purposes, he was in the country illegally.

The next day, while I was 'not getting involved,' Gerry managed to get himself into Indonesia legally, and change our flight to Bali for the following day. I never asked, and he never told me how that was accomplished. He also gave me Armando's correct telephone number and told me to "write it down!"

BALI

Bali was another experience in itself. We decided to tour the island by motorcycle, since we were motorcycle dealers. However, when they brought the motorcycle, it was not the large bike that we were expecting, but a 125cc, Honda's smallest motorcycle! We gamely got on the bike and started our tour.

Touring was not as bad as one would expect, mainly because we returned to our hotel every evening. We probably saw more of the island with the smaller bike. On Christmas Eve, we planned a trip that would take us to a dormant volcano where the Balinese 'buried' their dead above the ground. I had read about this place in National Geographic. We drove to the edge of the volcano and were told that we had missed the last ferry going to the site. Gerry, never accepting 'it can't be done' for an answer, decided to drive along the shore of the lake, which would get us closer to the site, and find someone with a boat. Well, we drove around the lake until we found someone who agreed to take us to the site. The 'boat' was a canoe, carved out of a log, but we were assured it was safe. Getting into the boat, the 'captain' put me in the front and had me hold our camera equipment and put Gerry in the rear. He then hopped in and pushed off. When the canoe got moving, he handed Gerry a paddle and a can. Halfway across the lake, I noticed that the canoe was leaking and told Gerry to start bailing!

We finally arrived at the site and took some pictures. The trip was worth it, as subsequently, the site was later declared a national memorial, with visitation limited. On our way back across the lake, a sudden storm arose, soaking us with water, and with winds that whipped the canoe from side to side. Fortunately, the leaking canoe was somewhat steady with not only our weight, but with the water in the bottom of it. We did not kiss the earth upon our arrival back at our motorcycle, but we certainly felt like doing just that!

As we were going down the side of the volcano, Gerry mentioned to me that we were almost out of gas. He said that he thought we passed a gas station back up the road, but he would not make it with me on the back. So, I got off the bike, and standing in the rain, in the middle of what seemed like a deserted village, I waited for Gerry to return.

I'm a dog lover. I presently have a Chesapeake Bay Retriever, and a Siberian Husky. So, when three or four village dogs approached me, I was not worried...until they started growling at me. It then occurred to me that this was not going to be a warm canine encounter.

Picking up some stones that were laying in the road and praying that I could throw them better than my encounter on that bridge in Turkey, I started throwing them at the dogs. Fortunately, they backed off just as Gerry came down the road. Continuing on our way, soaking wet and looking for a place to have a bowl of soup to warm us up, we agreed there were many other places where we could have spent Christmas Eve!

We finally found a place, on a lake, that was open and served soup. An hour later, our attitudes considerably better, we continued our way back to the hotel. The rain did not let up, and by the time we arrived back at the hotel, we were both so cold that we had to be helped off the motorcycle. We went back to our room, filled the bathtub with hot water, ordered hot tea with rum, and got in the tub fully clothed, to warm up. Merry Christmas!

Europe With Mom And Dad

About this time, Gerry got wanderlust again, and we decided that it would be an adventure if he got a job with Merrill Lynch in South America. We also decided in conjunction with this that we would meet my parents in Europe and give them the trip I had promised them when I returned from Europe in 1967. So, in the summer of 1975, we met my parents in London, and for the next 21 days, toured the continent.

Along the way, Gerry found out that Merrill Lynch would only hire him to work in English-speaking countries. The exception was, they would also send him to Russia. Since we had our minds set on South America, Gerry turned down the offer and we decided negotiating with Chrysler Military was our best bet.

July 17, 1975, we left Bangkok and flew to London via Bangladesh and Bahrain. In Bangladesh, we attempted to call our friends Tex and Marieta, who were Great Britain's Ambassadors to the country, but did not get through. All we accomplished was to get mud on our clothing. The country was under horrible storms and flooding. In Bahrain, I had my first contact with Islamic law in the form of women in purdah. At the time, seeing women fully hooded in black, head to toe, was very scary to me. After 12 hours, we arrived in London and crashed at the Sheraton Hotel.

The next morning, we took the hotel bus to the airport, and after experiencing a British 'slow down,' finally met my parents. We spent the entire day walking around London, having lunch at my old pub, The Black Swan, and visiting the American Express just to show my parents where I received mail when I lived in London in 1966.

While we were at American Express, a photographer came up to my parents and asked them if they wanted a picture. He told them that, for $20, he would take their picture and send it to them in the States. He took the picture with Mom holding my book, *Europe on 5 Dollars a Day*, and Dad gave him the $20 and their address in the States. For the rest of the vacation, Gerry teased my dad about being scammed in London. Dad got the last laugh, however, when he received the picture a month after arriving home! It was a gentler time in 1975.

The next day, we toured London by bus and got back to the hotel in time to change and arrive at the theater to see *No Sex Please, We're British*. I couldn't believe my mother fell asleep during the first act, but truth be told, I slept through the second act! Even though the play was neither funny nor interesting, to be fair, we were just tired!

The following day, we took a train to Dover, a ferry to Ostend, Belgium, rented a car, and drove to Amsterdam. The thing about the car was, after loading it with all our luggage, there was barely enough room for the four of us and we still had to pick up Gerry's mother in Germany! Arriving in Amsterdam, it took us an hour to find a hotel, check in, and haul our luggage up the notorious Dutch narrow stairways. However, the famous Dutch breakfasts did not disappoint.

After spending a day touring Amsterdam, we took off for Frankfurt, Germany. Chrysler Military Sales is headquartered in Frankfurt, and besides checking in and visiting old friends, Gerry intended to trade in our rental car for a VW CMSC Mini Van. With the mission accomplished, we drove to Fürth to have dinner with Gerry's mother.

The next day was spent visiting all of Gerry's relatives and friends, before leaving for Munich. It was so cold in Munich that we had to buy raincoats before going on our tours, the highlight of which was going to the Hofbrauhaus for beers and dinner, and the next day going to Salzburg, Austria, for dinner in the castle.

Taking off from Austria, we crossed the Alps on our way to Cortina d'Ampezzo. When we were in the Grossglockner Pass, we stopped to admire the view and give my father a respite from the mountain road. While we were stopped, a German approached Gerry and told him that it was an insult to have the word Chrysler Military on a VW van. Gerry asked him how long he had been on vacation, and he answered, "A month." Gerry explained that in the past month, Chrysler had taken over VW! We left the guy sputtering and mumbling to himself.

Crossing into Italy, we decided to stop at the first little town and spend the night, before going on to Venice. At dinner that night, my father, who was born in Italy, became very agitated reading the menu. When we asked why he said that he couldn't understand half of the menu. I told him that was because some of it was in German, which greatly relieved him.

The next day, we went on to Venice for lunch and a quick tour, and then left for Pievepelago, the town where my father was born. We were greeted by the townspeople as if we were royalty. Everybody had a story about my grandfather.

The following day, we walked around the town meeting all my father's relatives and my grandfather's friends. Gerry disappeared after breakfast with Marta, the town's old harlot, to have a picnic along the river. Since we were having dinner with all the relatives and friends, Dad and I decided to find Gerry at about 5pm, under the impression he may have imbibed too much. But as we walked around visiting, at every stop, we were offered a 'little sip' of homemade Strega. By the time we made the rounds and returned to the hotel, we frankly didn't care about finding Gerry. We had a great dinner, and halfway through, Gerry arrived, looking like he had been asleep in the bushes! Thankfully, he went right to our room and fell asleep.

After much hugging and kisses, we left for Florence, the town where I had lived in 1966. After checking into our hotel, we walked around the city. I wanted to show my parents where I used to hang out, but nothing was the same. Except, of course, the monuments! My favorite restaurant was now an electrical shop, selling things that weren't invented in 1966! We walked up Via de' Bardi, where I pointed out my apartment, but alas, it was now a restaurant! I took them to Piazza Michelangelo, for a view of the city which did not disappoint, giving way to the Italian expression "la bellissima cite del mondo (the most beautiful city in the world)."

We had a wonderful dinner and walked back down to the Red Garter. But instead of the banjo music played by my friends Wayne and John, there was a new group (of course, this was nine years later), who were hooked up to speakers, making conversation impossible. To top it off, my parents weren't impressed with the peanut shells on the floor. After one beer, we walked home.

The following day, we took a walking tour of Florence. I was excited. Unfortunately, as we walked down the street leading to the tower, we were stopped by the police. We were told that someone was on the top of the tower shooting at the police patrolling on horseback. I did get a photo of the terrorist and the tower, and we moved along to Piazza della Signoria for lunch. We never heard the end of the incident. I'm assuming the man was captured.

At 2pm, we left for Rome. In Rome, we did all the tourist things, visiting the Vatican, Saint Peter's Square, the Colosseum, the Roman Forum, everything that is Roman. After a nap, we went out for dinner, lucking out in finding a family-owned restaurant which was delicious, making for a wonderful evening.

The next day, we left for the French Riviera, stopping at Pisa, where we saw the Leaning Tower, and took all the tourist pictures. We bought some salami, cheese, and bread and had a picnic lunch overlooking the Mediterranean Sea. Deciding that we could not make it to Monaco, we stopped in Genoa for the night. We found a hotel in a little village in the Alps, had a nice dinner, and played Italian games before going to bed.

The next day, after a wonderful breakfast, we continued to Monaco, driving along the Riviera. Traffic was bumper to bumper as were the people on the beaches. Gerry made the comment, "If one person turns over, everyone will have to turn over!" Arriving in Monaco at 6pm, we barely had time to change for dinner.

Dinner at the Hotel de Paris was an interesting experience. At our waiter's recommendation, we ordered pâté as an appetizer. When it arrived, Gerry's mom said something in German, which Gerry translated. She thought the pâté tasted like Spam. At that, my father commented that he thought he recognized the taste. So much for an elegant French dinner!

The famous Monaco Casino was also a letdown, being a little run down. However, the view of the city from one of the hills above the city was spectacular at night.

Leaving early the next morning, we took off for Lyon where we had an 8pm dinner date with our friends from Saigon Cathy and Patrick. Again, traffic was bumper to bumper, so in Cannes, we got off the beach road and took the autoroute to Lyon. Checking in to the hotel Patrick had reserved, the registrar told us that he had three rooms but two of the rooms did not have a bathroom. We gave the room with a bathroom to Gerry's mother.

Gathering in the lobby before meeting with Cathy and Patrick, my parents informed us that they did, in fact, have a bathroom, but the toilet was broken. So, Dad fixed the toilet and Mom cleaned the sink and tub, prompting Gerry to remark that he intended to get a discount when we checked out in the morning! Lyon is famous for its kitchen and dinner did not disappoint; we had a great reunion with Cathy and Patrick, leaving the following day for Paris.

On the way, we intended to visit Gerry's roommate in Saigon, Peter. Peter had inherited a castle in Bligny, called Chateáu de Bligny. Included with the castle was a vineyard bottling Champagne. On the way, we cautioned our parents not to get too excited about seeing a castle—everyone in France claims to have a chateáu. Well, turns out Peter really did have a castle, with the two towers going back to the seventh century and the living quarters between the towers the fifteenth century. During WWII, the castle was used as a motor pool. The floor, which was marble, was torn up and thrown in the ravine behind the castle, since the marble didn't absorb the oil from the vehicles. Fortunately, Peter was able to salvage the marble for the floors, and in cleaning the walls from the diesel smoke, they found out they were covered with murals from the seventeenth century. It really was a castle.

We got a tour of the Champagne, from the grape crushers to the final bottling in the cellar. After spending a couple of hours reminiscing with Peter, drinking and buying excellent Champagne, we left for Paris.

The next day, we took an all-day tour of Paris, having breakfast in Mont Blanc and lunch at the Intercontinental Hotel. After the tour, the ladies went to the beauty parlor, and my father took a nap. Gerry and I bought tickets for the evening at the Moulin Rouge. The show at the Moulin Rouge was spectacular. A little bit naughty, but tastefully done. Gerry's Mom commented, "Some of those girls weren't so nice." My father agreed with her. But we all agreed it was way better than *No Sex Please. We're British.*

Heidelberg was our next stop. We checked into the hotel that Gerry's mom remembered as being the hotel where she stayed with Gerry's dad when they first moved to Germany from Canada. We went and looked at Heidelberg Castle, then had dinner at a guest house.

In the morning, we left for Fürth, as it was the end of the road for Gerry's mom. Even though she had been on the road with us for two weeks, she made a delicious early dinner. We said our goodbyes and drove to Frankfurt Airport where we turned over our car to a representative of CMSC and checked into the airport hotel. Not being hungry, we took a cab to Kaiser Strasse, had a beer in a beer hall, which was as noisy as the Red Garter, and called it a night.

The next day was the end of the road for Mom and Dad. The four of us flew to London, where Mom and Dad left for Chicago, and we left for Bangkok.

Upon our return to Thailand on August 9, CMSC offered us a position in the Republic of Panama. On August 17, we accepted it with an ETA of the seventeenth of September. That gave us a month to close out Thailand, ship what we wanted to keep, and sell the rest, including our two cars. We also went to the central market and bought all the things we always said we wanted. We went to Design Thai and bought bronze cutlery, to Thai Celadon to purchase a dinner set, and lamps, and to the frame shop to pick up the pictures we had framed.

On August 16, Bekins Movers came to pick up our household goods and we moved into the Dusit Thani Hotel, the same hotel we had lived in when we arrived in Bangkok. The next day, we caught a plane to Panama, stopping for two days in Hong Kong, to say goodbye to Asia, and two days in Mexico City to say hello to Central America.

REPUBLIC OF PANAMA

Gerry once had a boss whose motto was the following: "Beware of asking for things. You might get them and be sorry." The Republic of Panama was somewhat like that saying. Granted we eagerly accepted the assignment, but I guess being so close to the United States made us think of moving there and getting our own dealership. Panama to us was also a way of connecting. First and foremost, we met our partner and his wife, Walt and Rose. Walt was the manager of Chrysler International. My brother Tony came to visit and found his soulmate in our partner's daughter, Marla; and my sister Midge got to visit for two weeks and take a motorcycle trip to Costa Rica!

But the 15 months we spent in the Republic wasn't all work and planning to get out. We did have some memorable experiences.

Our first was a panicked call from Larry, one of our salesmen from Thailand, who told Gerry that he had arrived, but he was in Panama City, Florida, not the Republic of Panama! Just a minor bit of miscommunication. The next little stumble was the fact that we had shipped our 6,000 pounds of household goods to the Canal Zone, not realizing that we needed paperwork to get them out of the bonded warehouse and into the Republic of Panama. This problem was solved when Gerry met a fellow Canadian, Hart, who had ridden to the Republic of Panama from Canada on a Harley-Davidson. Together with the Harley-Davidson Gerry had, compliments of Chrysler, the two rode into the Canal Zone's bonded warehouse at 7:30 on Thanksgiving morning, waved some papers at the gate, and loaded up our household goods on a borrowed truck. The whole operation took one-and-a-half hours!

We arrived in the Republic of Panama on September 21, 1975. Because we had spent 22 days in Europe with Mom and Dad, we decided to spend Christmas in Panama. Specifically camping with the motorcycle club in David, which was in the mountainous region of Panama. We were going to spend two days camping in the Hinklins' yard, a retired Canal Zonian and his wife, who had a soft spot for the motorcycle club. As it turned out, seven miles from the Hinklins', RT's motorcycle went into a high-speed wobble and he wiped out, breaking a couple of ribs. Since there were only four of us, Gerry, me, RT, and his wife, Jan, and RT was hurt, Mrs. Hinklin graciously invited us to stay as guests of theirs, which made it a far better Christmas than sleeping in a tent! The joke of the trip was the fact that RT, the whole week before, kept saying he was going to drive to David and crash, but not literally!

The year 1976 started off with a visit from Arnold, Gerry's boss, sales manager for Asia and the Caribbean, and the best man at our wedding. It was significant in that he finally made me the administrator of Panama with an agreed-upon salary, and gave me authorization to hire a secretary! Gerry, on the other hand, was given Puerto Rico to manage along with Panama, which meant traveling every five or six weeks to Puerto Rico. It was after his first trip to Puerto Rico that he decided that he would rather have his own dealership than put up with the hassle of working for someone else.

I did get to visit my family for three days on my way to a business trip in New York in February. The purpose of the trip was for the New York office to understand the needs of the field. But no matter how eloquently I described these needs, the New York office personnel still felt that all we in the field did was party all day and play all night. It was a lost cause and only added to the burn of leaving the company and getting our own dealership somewhere in the States.

One incident that we laugh about now but wasn't so funny at the time was the 'catalytic converter affair.' All cars made in the United States were and are equipped with catalytic converters, which allows for lead-free gasoline. At the time, 1976, Panama did not have lead-free gas. So, when one of our cars came into Panama, the catalytic converter had to be removed. When the car was then shipped back to the States, the converter was reinstalled. The depository for all these converters was a big box in my office. The problem was, we could never seem to match up the converter with the car going back to the States!

Another fact of having in-country deliveries was it took longer for a car to be shipped the 60 miles from Cristobal, the port of entry, to the Chrysler dealer in Panama City by train, than it took for the car to be shipped from Miami to Cristobal by boat. This is too long for an impatient person, and one day we dealt with just such an individual.

She came barging into my office as I was interviewing a potential employee, demanding to know where her car was. I politely explained how the automotive supply line worked and even had my interviewee repeat the explanation in Spanish, but she was not appeased and started yelling, "My car or my money!" She then proceeded to clear off my desk to make her point. My interviewee decided the job was not for him and got up to leave. As he excused himself and walked past her, she almost knocked him down. Just then, the phone rang. It was the Chrysler International office down the hall. They asked me if they should call the police, and I told them yes. Sensing that something was up, my impatient customer said something to the effect that she would 'show us' and ran out of the office. The secretary from Chrysler International called again and told me they knew this customer and she was dangerous. They told me to lock the door.

The next thing I knew, I heard gunshots. She had returned, and when she found the door locked, she started shooting at the door. It was ironic. Five years in Vietnam during the war, and I was now being shot at in the relatively peaceful Republic of Panama. Just then, the police came, told the woman to leave, and cautioned us not to upset her again. It seemed she was the mayor's wife!

Towards the end of February, Midge came for a visit. Because this was the first time she had ever visited us, we really wanted to show her around, and as a result, we got to see and do new things too. We rented a boat and went fishing on Lake Gatun, rented a power boat and visited some islands in the Perlas chain, stopping to sunbathe on Taboga, and went on a motorcycle trip to Costa Rica. Costa Rica was famous for its oxcarts and leather. Midge and I bought oxcarts—she, a little one that sits on her shelf, and me, a big one that is a piece of furniture. Gerry bought a beautiful leather duffel bag, which we have to this day.

Our next visitor was the administrator of Chrysler Military Sales, Paul. His trip was in exchange for my trip to New York. Our mission was, again, to prove to him that life in the field wasn't all roses. So, without planning it, on his second night in Panama, as we were returning from dinner, a car hit ours. As Gerry was taking down the driver's driving license number, a man ran up, claiming his car was hit too! The next day, Paul went to the bank to present a letter of credit and was almost arrested for taking pictures. Paul went back to New York with the impression that living 'abroad' was a bit dangerous. Mission accomplished!

Chrysler Military Sales represented Chrysler, Plymouth, and Dodge as well as Harley-Davidson motorcycles. Since I had always wanted to learn to drive a motorcycle, well, more like a Vespa, I decided to learn in Panama. The guy who put our motorcycles together when they arrived in Panama was a police officer in the Canal Zone. He offered to teach me if I agreed to drive one of his motorcycles to David, where he had it sold. The plan was for the motorcycle club to take another trip to David and I would come back with Gerry on his motorcycle. Gerry wasn't a fan of this plan because the motorcycle was an FLH 1200cc bike. He agreed, only if I proved that I could drive the bike. Gerry went on another trip to Puerto Rico, and I practiced.

April 9 was D-Day. I left with Jerry, my teacher, at 11:25 from the Canal Zone and we got to David around 8pm. Gerry followed with RT and Jan, who by the way had her own FLH, arriving two hours later. I wrote in my day planner that I didn't fall once. When someone asked Gerry why he didn't travel with me, he admitted he was afraid I would fall.

In June, with Chrysler's consent, we took a trip to Lake Forest and then on to Los Angeles via motorcycle. Gerry left a week early, stopping off in Puerto Rico for a few days to work with the men there, before flying to Lake Forest. He then flew to York, Pennsylvania, to pick up a new 1976 edition Harley-Davidson.

Six days later, I joined Gerry in Lake Forest. Because we were going on a cross-country trip, I packed in cardboard boxes. This was back in the days when you dressed up to travel, so arriving in Miami in my linen suit and silk blouse with two cardboard boxes raised a bell with the custom officials. When I told the officials that I was going on a motorcycle trip and had to fit my clothes in two saddle bags, they let me go.

Lake Forest was a happy reunion of the Vignocchi family and Gerry's mother. We celebrated the Fourth of July all together, having a great time with the help of Gerry's sangria at the evening fireworks. We went to Champaign-Urbana to visit the University of Illinois, and to Ravinia for Unity Day. We were able to have a wonderful Mexican dinner, compliments of Maria, who my mother referred to as her Mexican friend because she was more than household staff. Then, we spent a day in Chicago, having dinner at Gino's, home of the Chicago deep-dish pizza.

We left on our motorcycle trip on July 10. First stop was Des Moines, Iowa, where we visited my cousins Bob and Alice. As we were leaving the next day, the windshield on the Harley started cracking. By the following day, it was evident we would have to stop and have it fixed or replaced. On our way after replacing the windshield, and just as we crossed over the Colorado state line, we got what seemed like a flat tire, and the bike started to wobble. Gerry told me he was going to lay the bike down on the left so I should be prepared to jump off. All I could think of was that I would not make it and the bike would take off my left leg, and Gerry would leave me because I was disabled!

So, I talked Gerry down, telling him I was sure he could keep the bike upright as it came to a stop. Mission accomplished but Gerry said we did not have a flat tire; 13 spokes had let loose, and we would have to buy a new wheel. As we were assessing the damages, a young man with a pickup stopped to help and we were able to load the Harley into the bed of his truck. This was a Monday and traditionally motorcycle shops are closed on Mondays, but the young man told us that he knew of an unauthorized Harley shop.

When we got to the shop, the mechanic told us the first thing he had to do was take the tire off the wheel. When he was unable to break the seal, he asked Gerry and the young man to stand on one side of the wheel and he would jump on the other side. This was necessary because, at the time, Gerry only weighed 155 pounds, the young man was thinner, and the mechanic must have weighed at least 400 pounds! As the mechanic jumped on one side of the tire, Gerry and the young man flew off the tire. The seal was not broken. Gerry suggested that, maybe, if the pickup truck drove halfway over the tire, it would break the seal. This bent the wheel, really making it unfixable, but it also broke the seal.

Gerry noticed that in the back of the shop was another Harley FLH. Gerry suggested that he could buy the wheel and the mechanic could then buy another wheel when the Harley shop opened the next day. The mechanic said that the bike belonged to a doctor in town, so Gerry asked for his number. When he called, the doctor's wife told Gerry the doctor was hunting somewhere in Mexico and wouldn't be back for a week. So, doing one of the things Gerry did best, he was able to track down the doctor and asked if he could buy the wheel. The doctor said yes, the problem was solved, and the mechanic got underway taking the wheel off the doctor's bike and putting it on ours.

We had the accident at 2:30pm and didn't get back on the road until 8pm. Just as we got to Loveland, before going over the pass, it started to rain. Figuring the elements were against us, we called it quits for the day and found a motel across the street from an Italian restaurant. The server told us the restaurant really belonged to his daughter and her husband and he and his wife were 'restaurant sitting' while the couple were in Europe. Consequently, the only thing the restaurant was serving was pizza, so we ordered a pizza and a pitcher of beer. After our day, we were dehydrated, so we quickly finished off the pitcher of beer before the pizza arrived and ordered another one.

Finally, the pizza arrived, and Gerry reached for the container of red pepper flakes. As he turned the container upside down to shake some flakes on the pizza, the top came off and emptied the contents on our pizza. The couple came running over and immediately offered to fix us another pizza. We said that we would make do but after taking a bite realized that the pizza was inedible, so we ordered another pizza and another pitcher of beer. Walking back to the motel after dinner, we both realized we had to urgently use the bathroom. Gerry, being a gentleman, let me go first. Upon exiting the bathroom, I closed the door and told Gerry it was his turn. Gerry went to the bathroom, but the door would not open. When he rattled the doorknob, it fell off. Desperate, he went out to the Harley and took out his tool bag. He proceeded to take the door off its hinges, but the door still would not open. I ran to the office and told the man at the desk our problem. He laughed and said, "Oh, that door never opens," and gave me a coat hanger to use in the door. Well, that worked but after that we always made sure the door remained open (and yes, Gerry put the door back on its hinges!).

The next day, we drove through Estes Park and on to Salt Lake City. As we approached Heber City, the chain on the motorcycle started knocking. Gerry tightened it, but it still knocked, forcing us to stop for the night. When Gerry inspected the chain, he discovered the chain guard was broken. Up early the next morning, we got the guard fixed, and we proceeded on to Salt Lake City. Stopping only to see the Tabernacle and Chapel, we continued to Reno, Nevada, in time to see the sunset, shower and change, and have a nice dinner and a drink. We found a bar where you could drink and gamble without getting off the barstool. We gambled until 3am and walked out of the bar with the money we came in with. No wins and no losses.

The next day, it was on to Los Angeles through the Sierra Mountains. It was a beautiful ride until we crossed the Oakland Bay Bridge. It started getting cold and the further down the coast we went, the colder it got. We stopped for coffee and pie, a nice interlude. Gerry grabbed all the free newspapers and zipped them into his jacket for warmth. Our destination was visiting San Simeon, Hearst Castle. Arriving too late for a tour, much to my disappointment and Gerry's elation, I suggested that we do it the next time we were in California, and we did, 23 years later!

We spent the night in Morro Bay, arriving at the motel so cold that we could hardly get off the motorcycle—shades of Christmas Eve in Bali 1974! The next day, we arrived in LA and gladly dropped off the bike, changed, repacked and caught a 7:50 flight to San Antonio to visit our friends Stewart and Jan.

San Antonio was an eye opener for Gerry and me. We had a chance to see how great living in the US could be. Stewart and Jan took us to lunch and waterskiing on a nearby lake. The next day, we went to a couple of ranches to meet some of their friends, ending up BBQing at their home that evening. Piña coladas were all the rage, and we decided to make some for cocktail hour. We went to the store to buy cream of coconut, but being Sunday, the only thing open was a little market that did not have cream of coconut but had coconuts. I came up with the idea that if we blended the coconuts, it would be just as good as the cream of coconut. We blended the coconuts, added pineapple juice, and rum, and voilà, a piña colada that you had to chew! Not one of my better ideas!

The day after, we said goodbye to Stewart and Jan. We flew to Houston, where we rented a car and drove to Clear Lake to look at a dealership Walt had found, then on to Panama via Miami. By the way, when Jerry picked up the motorcycle, being a mechanic, he diagnosed its problem as an unbalanced flywheel and made Harley-Davidson pay for all the repairs we had incurred on the way to LA and those he had driving the thing back to Ohio!

On September 14, we officially accepted a deal in Bradenton, Florida, for a motorcycle dealership, with our partners, Walt and Rose. We were looking for a car dealership, but every one we looked at had problems we weren't willing to buy into. Especially the one in Connecticut, where we would have had to pay the 'mafia' $250,000 before negotiating the deal! And the one in Oklahoma where the bank told us we could get a floor plan for our cars if it rained, and the crops were good.

They say everything happens for a reason: the next day, the US Embassy put all Americans on alert. Seems the Panamanian government had accused the CIA of causing unrest and riots. It was like Vietnam all over again! Time to go. But it wasn't until the end of October that leaving became a reality. First, Gerry had to fly to New York to turn over all the sensitive files, the orders for October, and accompany our best, and most difficult salesman, David, who quit when he heard we were leaving Panama.

The day after Gerry left, I received a phone call from a representative of TWA that Gerry had left his briefcase in the taxi the day before. The caller gave me the telephone number of the taxi driver. I asked him how he tracked me down and he told me there was a business card in the briefcase of the man we had turned the motorcycle over to in LA, who had a brother who lived in the Canal Zone, who knew one of our salesmen, who gave him my number. I couldn't wait for the next day to call the New York office and tell Gerry he had left his briefcase in the taxi. That briefcase had $2500 in cash deposits with the orders and Gerry's passport, and all the taxicab driver did was call TWA and report it. The taxi driver was richly rewarded.

A few days later, Chrysler's packers came and packed up everything we were sending to the States, 6,000 pounds of not furniture but everything we had collected in the eight years we lived overseas.

In preparation for leaving, since we intended to drive to the States through Central America, Gerry purchased a van from Chrysler and had it converted into a mini camper. We had a bed in the back; it was fully carpeted and had a liquor cabinet on one of the doors. He also had a picture of the Panama City waterfront painted on one of the sides. The van was bluebird sky blue, so the panorama of the waterfront was really a work of art. It was also the first vehicle Gerry had purchased in his adult life (except for the Porsches he raced in Europe, and the one he bought in Canada when he was 14 years old), always having company vehicles to drive. In the middle of November, we went about selling what was left. But unlike Asia, when we had our house sale to get rid of everything we weren't taking to Panama, people did not flock to our house. We had to get creative, so we made a list of everything we wanted to sell, put an ad in the English paper, and mailed 180 lists to everyone in the business community. At last, success! On November 30, we were finally able to move out of the apartment and into the Allbrook officer's BOQ.

We lived in the BOQ for 16 days, working every day tying up loose ends, training the secretary to do my job, and supporting Gerry's replacement, Mike, the salesman from Vietnam, whose talent was to stand on his head on a bar and drink a beer! We also took time to visit with our Canal Zone friends, play a little golf, and do a little fishing. We finally left Panama on December 17, hitting the middle of the Bridge of the Americas at 3pm.

CENTRAL AMERICA

Our first stop along the way was to say goodbye to our friends in David, Rocky and Tati. We had two days of great food, visited Rocky's parents' farm in the Volcan, sipped brilliant Spanish rosé, talked, and listened to Rocky play the guitar. We also stopped in Durango to say goodbye to the Hinklins.

On the nineteenth, we left David and crossed the border into Costa Rica and drove to Puntarenas for the night. The next day, we made it to Nicaragua. We drove to Managua, the capital city, and were shocked to see that because of an earthquake years before there was basically no city left, only the outskirts! Moving on, we got to the Nicaraguan–Honduras border at 6pm but had to wait until the customs officials finished their dinner. "Benvenuti a America Centrale!" Clearing customs, we drove to Choluteca where our hotel compared to the best that Saigon had to offer, which is to say it wasn't much, but it did have security for our van.

We made it to the El Salvadorian border by 11:30am the following day. This was our most expensive border in terms of bribe money; it was $8.00. Excuse me. Not bribe money but payment for Feliz Navidad! When we were saying goodbye to Rocky, he gave us a letter of introduction for his roommate in dental school who lived in San Salvador. He told us we would be most welcome to stay with him and his family there. Not wanting to be put in that position, we opted not to look up Rocky's friend but did stop in the market and bought a sword.

I told Gerry I saw a sign for a Mayan ruin, so we took a detour off the Pan-American Highway and ended up in the Cerro Verde National Park. It was getting late, and we saw a sign for a hotel, so we turned on the road to the hotel. Halfway up the mountain, the road was unpaved and consisted of large rocks. Gerry panicked that the rocks were going to wreck the paint job on the van, but it was getting dark, and we were committed to getting to this hotel. When we finally found the hotel, it was worth the trip as it was level with the Volcano Izalco, known as the torch light of the Pacific. We watched the sunset over martinis and as it got dark, the volcano began sputtering fiery lava, thus proving its reputation.

We met the only other couple in the dining room and got to talking with them about where they were from and how they ended up at this hotel. They told us that they were from San Salvador and were on their honeymoon. According to them, the hotel, Escuela Cerro Verde, was a school for waiters and the only people who came to it were high government officials and people in power. They said the honeymoon was a gift from the girl's godfather. That explained why, for pennies, we had a three-room suite. We invited them back to our room for coffee and cognac, and over the evening, we discovered that our letter of introduction was to the girl's godfather. Small world. We gave the letter to them, to give to her godfather, and told her to tell him that timewise, we couldn't stop! A good time was had by all!

The next day, we continued to see the Tazumal ruins but ended up taking the wrong road which took us to the other side of Izalco Volcano.

Gerry commented, "Well, I wanted to see it one more time, anyway!"

Giving up, we crossed into Guatemala, with the intention of going to Antigua. Taking the wrong road, we ended up in Guatemala City.

Making lemonade out of lemons, we took a quick tour of the city and ended up finding a road sign for Antigua.

On our way, I saw another sign for the San Andreas Mayan ruins. I convinced Gerry to stop. Unfortunately, we ended up in the middle of a sugar cane field on our way to the ruins. Gerry got all agitated, claiming the crops the van was brushing against were ruining the special paint job we had on the van. In this mood, he proclaimed, the ruins, when we found them, were "nothing but a worthless pile of rocks."

We finally arrived at Antigua, a beautiful old city, and we luckily found a beautiful hotel, La Posada de Don Rodrigo, that used to be an old villa. Gerry even found a garage for his precious van! We had a great evening.

The next day, we drove to San Antonio de las Aguas Calientes, famous for weaving. We bought a rug and some material from Caroline, who had a weaving certificate from Germany! From there, we drove to Chichicastenango, which is an Indigenous market town. After buying a blanket and a mask, we continued to Huehuetenango to visit the Zaculeu ruins.

Thinking that we could continue on the dirt road into Mexico, we ended up on the bank of a dried-up river instead, where we met two Swiss boys. They were on their way to Tierra del Fuego, the tip of South America, having just driven from New York, where they had bought their camper. They showed us the dirt road we needed to take to get to Mexico, but since it was almost 7pm, we decided to camp right on the riverbed. We combined our food and drinks (remember our liquor cabinet on the door of the van) and had a raucous good time.

The next day, we followed the dirt road north and finally made it to Mexico. The easiest border crossing yet. Although the customs officials made me throw away my lemon. It seems fresh fruit is not allowed in Mexico. Shortly after entering Mexico, we found ourselves driving through the Sierra Madre mountains. The views were beautiful. The driving was slow. Finally, at about 6:30, we entered a town with a hotel.

Unfortunately, the rooms were not to our liking (lots of cockroaches), so we decided to sleep in the van for the second night. It was December 24, not the way I wanted to spend Christmas Eve.

Promising ourselves that we would find a better town to spend Christmas in, we took off for Oaxaca. Upon arrival, we first secured a hotel, took showers, and then walked around the town, ending up in the Zócalo (town square). We had dinner at an outdoor restaurant, good food and great Christmas lights. Up early the next day, we went to the market and bought ice, bread, and cheese. We read in our guidebook that Oaxaca was famous for its string cheese, and it did not disappoint. The cheese was delicious, and to date, four decades later, I have yet to find any string cheese to compare. After touring the town and taking pictures, we took off for Puebla.

Puebla was another town that did not disappoint. We found a hotel right on the Zócalo and had dinner again at an outdoor restaurant. The next morning, we walked around the town, visiting the Chapel del Rosario of Santo Domingo. This church's altar was covered completely in gold, most impressive. We then took off for Cholula and the ruins, which were also very impressive, the largest in Mexico.

Getting on the Pacific Highway, on our way to San Juan Teotihuacán, to see the Pyramid of the Sun and the Moon, we ended up in Mexico City. After a heated discussion of how to get out of Mexico City, we finally found the highway, ending up on a clover leaf which went north and south. Unfortunately, it seemed that no matter which way we took, we ended up at the same toll booth. Forty-five minutes and 22 pesos later, we finally got ourselves heading north towards the USA.

Driving until we almost ran out of gas, we finally got to Zimapan, a town with a gas station and a hotel. The hotel, Fundicion, which means foundry, was in an old foundry. While eating dinner, we made friends with the owner and his German manager. As the evening got later, a very tall Indian entered the restaurant and sat down with the owner.

Not realizing that Gerry was fluent in German, the three men began conducting business, which consisted of the owner paying a bribe to the very tall Indian on behalf of the mayor for the privilege of doing business. With that, we decided it was bedtime.

Up early the next morning, the object of the day was to 'make tracks' to the USA the most expedient way. Along the way, we passed the town of Linares, which our guidebook described as a "charming little town." We decided this was code for dusty! We spent the night about 250 miles from the border at a charming hotel called the Escondido, owned by a Mexican and his American wife. Dinner was good, but the night was cold, and although the bed in our room was too narrow to sleep together, it was too cold not to!

Finally, at noon, on December 29, 1976, we finally arrived in Nuevo Loredo, the border town between Mexico and the USA. We had driven a total of 3,800 miles from the Bridge of the Americas to the US border.

Crossing the border was easy back in those days; we simply showed the border officials our passports and drove across. However, Gerry was officially immigrating, so he had to go into the immigration building and get a green card. This took about one-and-a-half hours. I kept being told to move on, and I repeatedly told the officials that I was waiting for my husband to immigrate. Their reply was always, "Oh, the blond!"

Finally entering the USA, we called our friends Jan and Stewart and were told that they were hunting in Mexico! It seems everybody goes to Mexico to hunt! So, driving to San Antonio, we met up with a couple we had met in Aspen while skiing in 1974. After spending two days visiting our friends and San Antonio, we left very early on the thirty-first towards our destination and future, Bradenton, Florida.

We only got as far as the Holiday Inn in Crestview, Florida that first day but arriving in Florida on December 31 qualified us for counting 1976 as year one towards Florida's Homestead Law of five years in-state to take the deduction, when we ultimately bought our first home.

We met up with our partners, Walt and Rose, on January 2, 1977. Two things will forever be etched in my mind. First, possibly the first time in anyone's memory, it started to snow! And second, while having breakfast at Kissin' Cuzzins, we were met by my brother Tony and our partner's daughter, Marla, who announced their engagement.

Judy D.V. Harles